Praise for *The Best American Poetry*

"Each year, a vivid snapshot of what a distinguished poet finds exciting, fresh, and memorable: and over the years, as good a comprehensive overview of contemporary poetry as there can be."
—Robert Pinsky

"*The Best American Poetry* series has become one of the mainstays of the poetry publication world. For each volume, a guest editor is enlisted to cull the collective output of large and small literary journals published that year to select seventy-five of the year's 'best' poems. The guest editor is also asked to write an introduction to the collection, and the anthologies would be indispensable for these essays alone; combined with [David] Lehman's 'state-of-poetry' forewords and the guest editors' introductions, these anthologies seem to capture the zeitgeist of the current attitudes in American poetry."
—Academy of American Poets

"A high volume of poetic greatness . . . in all of these volumes . . . there is brilliance, there is innovation, there are surprises."
—*Publishers Weekly* (starred review)

"A year's worth of the very best!"
—*People*

"A preponderance of intelligent, straightforward poems."
—*Booklist*

"A 'best' anthology that really lives up to its title."
—*Chicago Tribune*

"An essential purchase."
—*The Washington Post*

"For the small community of American poets, *The Best American Poetry* is the *Michelin Guide*, the *Reader's Digest*, and the Prix Goncourt."
—*L'Observateur*

D0168370

OTHER VOLUMES IN THIS SERIES

John Ashbery, editor, *The Best American Poetry 1988*

Donald Hall, editor, *The Best American Poetry 1989*

Jorie Graham, editor, *The Best American Poetry 1990*

Mark Strand, editor, *The Best American Poetry 1991*

Charles Simic, editor, *The Best American Poetry 1992*

Louise Glück, editor, *The Best American Poetry 1993*

A. R. Ammons, editor, *The Best American Poetry 1994*

Richard Howard, editor, *The Best American Poetry 1995*

Adrienne Rich, editor, *The Best American Poetry 1996*

James Tate, editor, *The Best American Poetry 1997*

Harold Bloom, editor, *The Best of the Best American Poetry 1988–1997*

John Hollander, editor, *The Best American Poetry 1998*

Robert Bly, editor, *The Best American Poetry 1999*

Rita Dove, editor, *The Best American Poetry 2000*

Robert Hass, editor, *The Best American Poetry 2001*

Robert Creeley, editor, *The Best American Poetry 2002*

Yusef Komunyakaa, editor, *The Best American Poetry 2003*

Lyn Hejinian, editor, *The Best American Poetry 2004*

Paul Muldoon, editor, *The Best American Poetry 2005*

Billy Collins, editor, *The Best American Poetry 2006*

Heather McHugh, editor, *The Best American Poetry 2007*

Charles Wright, editor, *The Best American Poetry 2008*

David Wagoner, editor, *The Best American Poetry 2009*

Amy Gerstler, editor, *The Best American Poetry 2010*

Kevin Young, editor, *The Best American Poetry 2011*

Mark Doty, editor, *The Best American Poetry 2012*

Robert Pinsky, editor, *The Best of the Best American Poetry: 25th Anniversary Edition*

Denise Duhamel, editor, *The Best American Poetry 2013*

Terrance Hayes, editor, *The Best American Poetry 2014*

Sherman Alexie, editor, *The Best American Poetry 2015*

Edward Hirsch, editor, *The Best American Poetry 2016*

Natasha Trethewey, editor, *The Best American Poetry 2017*

Dana Gioia, editor, *The Best American Poetry 2018*

Major Jackson, editor, *The Best American Poetry 2019*

Paisley Rekdal, editor, *The Best American Poetry 2020*

THE

BEST

AMERICAN

POETRY

2021

◊ ◊ ◊

Tracy K. Smith, Editor

David Lehman, Series Editor

SCRIBNER POETRY

NEW YORK LONDON TORONTO SYDNEY NEW DELHI

Scribner Poetry
An Imprint of Simon & Schuster, Inc.
1230 Avenue of the Americas
New York, NY 10020

First Scribner edition September 2021

For information about special discounts for bulk purchases,
please contact Simon & Schuster Special Sales at 1-866-506-1949
or business@simonandschuster.com.

The Simon & Schuster Speakers Bureau can bring authors to your live event.
For more information or to book an event, contact the Simon & Schuster Speakers
Bureau at 1-866-248-3049 or visit our website at www.simonspeakers.com.

Manufactured in the United States of America

1   3   5   7   9   10   8   6   4   2

Library of Congress Control Number: 88644281

ISBN 978-1-9821-0662-1
ISBN 978-1-9821-0663-8 (pbk)
ISBN 978-1-9821-0664-5 (ebook)

CONTENTS

Foreword by David Lehman   xi

Introduction by Tracy K. Smith   xxi

Rosa Alcalá, "The Pyramid Scheme"   1

Lauren K. Alleyne, "Divination"   3

Jabari Asim, "Some Call It God"   5

Joshua Bennett, "Benediction"   7

Destiny O. Birdsong, "love poem that ends at popeyes"   10

Susan Briante, "Further Exercises"   13

Jericho Brown, "Work"   16

Christopher Buckley, "After Tu Fu"   18

Victoria Chang, "Marfa, Texas"   20

Chen Chen, "The School of Eternities"   22

Su Cho, "Abecedarian for ESL in West Lafayette, Indiana"   27

Ama Codjoe, "After the Apocalypse"   29

Henri Cole, "Gross National Unhappiness"   33

Billy Collins, "On the Deaths of Friends"   34

Adam O. Davis, "Interstate Highway System"   36

Kwame Dawes, "Before the Riot"   39

Toi Derricotte, "The Great Beauty"   41

Jay Deshpande, "A Child's Guide to Grasses"   43

Natalie Diaz, "lake-loop"   46

Alex Dimitrov, "Love"   49

Rita Dove, "Naji, 14. Philadelphia."   59

Camille T. Dungy, "This'll hurt me more"   60

Louise Erdrich, "Stone Love"   62

Kathy Fagan, "Conqueror"   64

Chanda Feldman, "They Ran and Flew from You"   65

Nikky Finney, "I Feel Good"   67

Louise Glück, "Night School"   69

Nancy Miller Gomez, "Tilt-A-Whirl"   71

Jorie Graham, "I Won't Live Long"   73

Rachel Eliza Griffiths, "Hunger"   76

francine j. harris, "Sonata in F Minor, K. 183: Allegro"   77

Terrance Hayes, "George Floyd"   78

Edward Hirsch, "Waste Management"   80

Ishion Hutchinson, "David"   82

Didi Jackson, "Two Mule Deer"   83

Major Jackson, "Double Major"   86

Amaud Jamaul Johnson, "So Much for America"   87

Yusef Komunyakaa, "Wheelchair"   88

Dana Levin, "Immigrant Song"   90

Ada Limón, "The End of Poetry"   92

James Longenbach, "In the Village"   93

Warren C. Longmire, "Meditations on a Photograph of Historic Rail Women"   97

Emily Lee Luan, "When My Sorrow Was Born"   99

Dora Malech, "All the Stops"   100

Sally Wen Mao, "Playing Dead"   102

Francisco Márquez, "Provincetown"   105

Hannah Marshall, "This Is a Love Poem to Trees"   107

Shane McCrae, "The Hastily Assembled Angel on Care and Vitality"   109

Lupe Mendez, "There Is Only You"   111

Francine Merasty, "Since Time Immemorial"   113

Yesenia Montilla, "a brief meditation on breath"   114

Kamilah Aisha Moon, "Irony"   116

Stanley Moss, "A Smiling Understanding"   117

dg nanouk okpik, "When White Hawks Come"   118

Cecily Parks, "December"   119

Patrick Phillips, "Elegy with Table Saw & Cobwebs"   121

Roger Reeves, "For Black Children at the End of the World—
and the Beginning" 123

Ed Roberson, "For Air" 125

Margaret Ross, "Blood" 127

Angbeen Saleem, "black and brown people on shark tank" 130

Nicole Sealey, "Pages 5–8" (An excerpt from *The Ferguson
Report: An Erasure*) 132

Evie Shockley, "women's voting rights at one hundred (but
who's counting?)" 139

Darius Simpson, "What Is There to Do in Akron, Ohio?" 142

Patricia Smith, "The Stuff of Astounding: A Golden Shovel for
Juneteenth" 144

Monica Sok, "Ode to the Boy Who Jumped Me" 146

Adrienne Su, "Chinese Restaurant Syndrome" 148

Arthur Sze, "Acequia del Llano" 150

Paul Tran, "Copernicus" 153

Phuong T. Vuong, "The Beginning of the Beginning" 154

John Sibley Williams, "The Dead Just Need to Be Seen. Not
Forgiven." 156

L. Ash Williams, "Red Wine Spills" 157

Shelley Wong, "How to Live in Southern California" 159

John Yau, "Overnight" 161

Monica Youn, "Caution" (*from* "Deracinations: Seven
Sonigrams") 163

Kevin Young, "Dog Tags" 167

Contributors' Notes and Comments 171

Magazines Where the Poems Were First Published 209

Acknowledgments 211

DAVID LEHMAN was born in New York City. Educated at Stuyvesant High School and Columbia University, he spent two years at Clare College, Cambridge, as a Kellett Fellow, and worked as Lionel Trilling's research assistant upon his return from England. His recent books include *One Hundred Autobiographies: A Memoir* (Cornell University Press, 2019), *Playlist: A Poem* (Pittsburgh, 2019), *Poems in the Manner Of* (Scribner, 2017), and *Sinatra's Century: One Hundred Notes on the Man and His World* (HarperCollins, 2015). He is the editor of *The Oxford Book of American Poetry* (2006) and *Great American Prose Poems: From Poe to the Present* (Scribner, 2003). In 2010, *A Fine Romance: Jewish Songwriters, American Songs* (Schocken) won the Deems Taylor Award from the American Society of Composers, Authors, and Publishers (ASCAP). Lehman launched *The Best American Poetry* series in 1988. A gathering of the forewords he had written for the series appeared in 2015 under the title *The State of the Art: A Chronicle of American Poetry, 1988–2014*. A contributing editor of *The American Scholar*, Lehman lives in New York City and in Ithaca, New York.

FOREWORD

by David Lehman

◊ ◊ ◊

Eleven of the poets who served as guest editors in this series went on to become U.S. Poet Laureate, or had already achieved the distinction, including this year's editor Tracy K. Smith. Our editors have won Pulitzers, National Book Awards, MacArthur and Guggenheim Fellowships. Two of them were named poetry editor of *The New Yorker*, which continues to be the premier periodical in which to place a poem. But not until this year did one win the most coveted prize of all, the Nobel, which Louise Glück (*BAP 1993*) received in October 2020.

I admire Louise's immediate response to the news, as reported in *Harper's*. Adam Smith, the chief scientific officer of Nobel Media, tried to interview her on the phone. When asked what the Nobel meant to her, Louise said, "I have no idea. My first thought was 'I won't have any friends' because most of my friends are writers." The interviewer persisted. How important is "lived experience"? "Oh, heavens," she said, "it's barely seven o'clock." Smith pressed on. "But it's so much a feature of your own writing?" Louise: "Is the two minutes over?"[1]

In her Nobel acceptance speech, Louise spoke up for the individuality and intimacy of the poetic act; it obeys imperatives that are private and not meant for the grandstand. "In art of the kind to which I was drawn, the voice or judgment of the collective is dangerous," she said. "The precariousness of intimate speech adds to its power and the power of the reader, through whose agency the voice is encouraged in its urgent plea or confidence." She aligned herself with those poets who "do not see reaching many in spatial terms, as in the filled auditorium. They see reaching many temporally, sequentially, many over time, into the future, but in some profound way these readers always come singly, one by one."[2]

1. "Prize Fighter," *Harper's* (January 2021), p. 17.
2. https://www.nobelprize.org/prizes/literature/2020/gluck/lecture/

Although I have devoted much energy to the project of enlarging the readership for poetry, I tend to agree that poetry is a solitary act, intimate and precarious. (The poet Stephen Paul Miller reminds me of an exchange he had with the late John Ashbery. "Do you think we can expand the audience for poetry?" Stephen asked. "Nah, let's keep it our little secret," John replied.) A poem is "a communication from one who is not the writer to one who is not the reader," Kenneth Koch rather mystically put it, attributing the statement to Paul Valéry. There does seem to be something mystical about the experience of communion with, for example, a poet who died a hundred years ago and wrote in a language you can read only at one remove. Louise Glück's distrust of the collective has never been less popular than it is at present, which makes the Nobel recognition all the more significant. I am happy to note that Louise continues to write and publish poems of note—such as "Night School," which the guest editor chose for *The Best American Poetry 2021*. It was wonderful to have something to celebrate in a year of plague, of anguish and woe without precedent for most of us.

So many died, lost a loved one, lost a job, made a sacrifice, paid a stiff price, or muddled through in a state of maximum uncertainty in 2020. We also went through a stunningly rapid upheaval in consciousness. Though there had been warnings, we were unprepared for a pandemic, perhaps because we have been distracted by such other disasters as forest fires, hurricanes, earthquakes, tsunamis, and the threat of bombs, missiles, terrorist attacks, volcanic eruptions, nuclear-plant meltdowns, and the geologic fate of the earth. COVID-19 was a killer the likes of which we had not encountered since World War II. By the first of March 2021 we had suffered half a million casualties in the United States alone, a shocking number of them in nursing homes. As the disease raged around the world, respecting no man-made borders, Dante's line, echoed by T. S. Eliot in *The Waste Land*, came to the fore: "I had not thought death had undone so many."

Overnight we went into a recession. The unemployment rate climbed to heights not seen since the Depression of the 1930s. In March the stock market collapsed, with the S&P 500 losing 34 percent of its value in just twenty-two trading sessions. Emergency conditions prevailed. Even after a strong mid-year rebound, the economy contracted 3.5 percent in 2020, the largest decline since just after World

War II.[3] Small stores shut their doors; famous companies sank. Hertz sold its fleet. Brooks Brothers went out of business. Restaurants died: after 157 years, the Cliff House in San Francisco closed its doors for good, as did the 21 Club in NYC. Airline stocks crashed, and conventional energy firms ran out of gas. Worst hit of all were the leisure and hospitality industries and those who work in them.

Not everyone liked the new restrictions imposed to limit the spread of the virus. People were urged—in some cases required—to wear masks in public places and to practice social distancing, with a mandatory six feet separating any two persons. Morale, shaky from the start, broke. Flagrant cases of police abuse sparked nationwide protests. The presidential election campaign upped the ante while lowering the civility index. Social media exacerbated mob impulses. On the federal, state, and local levels, governments faced unprecedented challenges, which they tried to meet with daily press briefings, massive relief and stimulus packages, the distractions of a permanent floating no-holds-barred political tag-team wrestling match, and Operation Warp Speed, a program to hasten the development of an effective vaccine. It seemed almost miraculous that, by late December, vaccines for a disease unknown twelve months earlier had won the approval of the Federal Drug Administration. A start-up outfit called Moderna was up there with Pfizer, Johnson & Johnson, and other major players in developing the treatment in record time.

The way we conduct our lives and our businesses rapidly changed. Satya Nadella, the highly regarded CEO of Microsoft, commented that "We've seen two years' worth of digital transformation in two months . . . in a world of remote everything." To the amazement of market watchers, stocks recovered in record time. The shares of disruptive technology firms, from Tesla to Zoom, were the rage. With so many able to work from home, the question was just how lasting will be the revolution in work habits.

Meanwhile the gap between rich and poor isn't narrowing, and the suffering of people, whether for medical or economic reasons, will persist no matter how massive a relief package Congress approves. The plague has delivered a devastating blow to so much that we value: theater, dance, orchestral and chamber music, cabarets, clubs, the opera.

3. Harriet Torry, "US Economy Suffers Worst Year Since '40s," *Wall Street Journal*, January 29, 2021, p. A1.

For the people out of work, the people who have had to close their businesses, the people who have lost a family member to the virus, the people who work (or used to work) at airports and hotels, restaurants, theaters, concert halls, and sports arenas—what, I wonder, can I, can any of us, do as poets?

For poets who teach or work at universities, the pandemic will have profound consequences. Some trends have accelerated, and for those of us who love books, not just the contents but the physical object, from cover to colophon, the idea of reading Proust or Henry James on a smartphone remains an incongruity and becomes a more pressing headache.

Many of us kept journals of the plague year. The wisdom of staying at home, restricting my social life and my contact with the world beyond nature, prompted me to renew an old habit and write a poem a day, which I began doing on August 1st. Three months earlier I had begun to struggle with the old subjects of doubt, chance, and gambling as sometimes an impulse, sometimes an imperative, and sometimes, alas, an addiction. I had never before felt so strongly that writing a poem was a gamble—with odds only somewhat better than that of a message in a bottle tossed into the ocean. Nevertheless, the act of writing a poem a day is one way of pushing back against an out-of-control world in which one's own volition counts for so little, and I keep doing it.

As a native of New York City, I can't help invoking a special prayer for the beleaguered city. I have in mind a paragraph in "Here is New York," a piece E. B. White wrote on assignment for Roger Angell, his editor at *Holiday* magazine, in 1949. "A poem compresses much in a small space and adds music, thus heightening its meaning," White wrote. "The city is like poetry: it compresses all life, all races and breeds, into a small island and adds music and the accompaniment of internal engines. The island of Manhattan is without any doubt the greatest human concentrate on earth, the poem whose magic is comprehensible to millions of permanent residents but whose full meaning will always remain elusive."

★

The series editor of *The Best American Poetry* has a multitude of jobs to do, but undoubtedly the most important is selecting the right person to be the year's guest editor—and getting her or him to say yes. The task of selecting seventy-five poems from the plethora of print and electronic magazines in which poems circulate is far from easy, and I am delighted that Tracy K. Smith agreed to take it on. There are personal reasons beyond the obvious literary ones. Between her undergraduate years at Harvard and her appointment as a Stegner Fellow at Stanford, Tracy studied at Columbia, and she was a star student in a graduate seminar I gave in spring 1996. The subject was the New York School of poets, and her expert imitation of a Kenneth Koch poem was so good that I sent it on to Richard Burgin, who published it in his magazine *Boulevard*. So it was and continues to be with particular joy that I have followed the flourishing of Tracy's career. *The Body's Question* (2003) was awarded the Cave Canem prize for the best first book by an African-American poet. *Duende* appeared four years later, and *Life on Mars* (2011) won her a Pulitzer. Smith's most recent book is *Wade in the Water* (2018). She has also written a memoir, *Ordinary Light* (2015).

In June 2017, Tracy became U.S. Poet Laureate. To accompany her on visits to community centers, she compiled an anthology, *American Journal: Fifty Poems for Our Time* (2018), in the hope of reaching readers who have never given poetry a chance. During the pandemic, she was one of four poets who celebrated National Poetry Month (April) by choosing among submissions solicited for *All Things Considered* on NPR.

Above all else, Tracy K. Smith is a distinguished practitioner of the art. Consider her poem "Ash." The title is either ominous or ironic or both. Using a loose, irregular rhyme scheme, and the force of repetition, Smith converts the humble "house" from essential domicile to multiple metaphor:

> Strange house we must keep and fill.
> House that eats and pleads and kills.
> House on legs. House on fire. House infested
> With desire. Haunted house. Lonely house.
> House of trick and suck and shrug.
> *Give-it-to-me* house. *I-need-you-baby* house.
> House whose rooms are pooled with blood.
> House with hands. House of guilt. House
> That other houses built. House of lies
> And pride and bone. House afraid to be alone.
> House like an engine that churns and stalls.

House with skin and hair for walls.
House the seasons singe and douse.
House that believes it is not a house. [4]

If the poem is an architectural wonder that could house us all, its fate and ours can, like the piece of paper on which it was written, go up in smoke and leave only ash behind. My friend Jamie Katz, the writer and jazz aficionado, pinned this poem to his refrigerator door after it appeared in print. "I was so struck by this poem," he said, "written in the present tense but freighted with history, mixing memory and desire, guilt and fear, sex and cruelty—such a visceral poem, concrete and direct, with a strong rhythm pushing it forward, which only adds to its urgent and pleading tone. And yes, why 'Ash'? Is this a house that has already burned down but remains alive in obsessive recall, or perhaps a place—real or imagined—that Smith wishes she could obliterate but can't, because her own life is so bound up in it? And who is the 'we' in the first line? Are we all implicated?"

Smith says she is "most interested in the marginal or overshadowed perspectives, the stories that sit outside of or beneath the central American narrative, or the accepted myths of American identity." That editorial philosophy is consistent with an impulse toward inclusiveness, as the contents of this volume confirm. "I know that who I am—a woman, African American, American, born in the late 20th Century and reckoning with life in the early 21st, etc.—has guided me toward the voices, stories, places, possibilities that interest and preoccupy me," Tracy told an interviewer from *Stay Thirsty*.[5] When asked why she chose to express herself in poetry rather than in prose, Tracy answered: "Poetry feels sacred to me, even when it is playful, secular, gritty. Poetry feels like the syntax of the unconscious mind, or—better still—the soul. I love prose, I write in other forms, but I believe that poetry unites me with my largest, perhaps my eternal self."

On January 20, 2021, a day filled with speeches and solemn oaths, the youngest inaugural poet in American history stole the show. Amanda Gorman, twenty-two, who graduated from Harvard in June 2020, boldly and with perfect poise recited her poem "The Hill We

4. The poem appeared in *The New Yorker*, November 23, 2015.
5. https://staythirstymagazine.blogspot.com/p/tracy-k-smith-conversation.html

Climb." The better verb would be "performed," for Amanda knew the poem as well as an actor knows her lines, and she delivered it with a winning confidence, using hip-hop rhythms and rhyme to excellent effect—commanding the audience rather than retreating from it, as some poets instinctively do. In the poem she read, she pictures herself as "a skinny Black girl / descended from slaves and raised by a single mother," who had (and may still have) a "dream of becoming president." She gave voice to the theme of unity: "We close the divide because we know, to put our future first, / we must first put our differences aside." In a reference to the riots at the Capitol on January 6, she wrote, "while democracy can be periodically delayed, / it can never be permanently defeated." The sentiments were lofty if familiar; the rhymes appealed to the ear, and the presentation won listener's hearts.

One day later, Penguin Children's announced that "due to overwhelming demand" it would publish a special hardcover edition of the "The Hill We Climb" with a first printing of 150,000 copies. By the twenty-eighth of January, the publication date was moved up to March 16 and the first printing elevated to one million copies. It was also announced that Oprah Winfrey would write a foreword for the book and that Gorman would write a poem for delivery at the Super Bowl in February. She planned to celebrate the game's three honorary captains: an educator, a nurse manager, and a Marine Corps veteran.

The emergence of Amanda Gorman as an overnight sensation was without doubt the poetry event of the year. She didn't exactly come out of nowhere. She introduced Hillary Clinton at the 2017 Global Leadership Awards, was celebrated by Michelle Obama at the White House, and opened for Tracy K. Smith at the Library of Congress. How did all this happen for the Los Angeles native? It goes back to 2017, when she was named America's National Youth Poet Laureate, the first to earn that designation. Growing out of programs on the local and state level, the National Youth Poet Laureate was an initiative undertaken by the Urban Word, a New York outfit headed by Michael Cirelli, himself a talented poet and a pedagogic innovator. Influenced by the spoken-word movement and the idea that performance and presentation are and should be integral to the creative process, Cirelli believes that literary excellence is compatible with political engagement. "We're still a tiny organization, but we built this huge platform for young poets in their teenage years," he told me with pride and a trace of awe. To identify "the best poets and the ones most invested in social impact," the Urban Word employs a group of judges to choose among four finalists aged fourteen to nineteen, who must submit a poetry portfolio, a CV, a video in which they introduce themselves, and an essay stating what they would do if selected. It is an annual appointment. In 2020, the fourth in the series was named: sixteen-year-old Meera Dasgupta of New York, whose commitment to social change—a requisite—is to the causes of gender equality and climate change. As to the success of the first National Youth Poet Laureate, Cirelli jokes that Amanda Gorman's "bio goes out of date every two weeks," so swift has been her climb, so charismatic her personality, so fierce her energy and determination.

From the start, this anthology series has acted on the belief that many varieties, schools, and movements of poetry can coexist and even flourish in a shared space. I take "unity" in the larger context to mean the same sort of respect and tolerance; the sense, too, that all of us are greater than the sum of our opinions; and the conviction that disagreements, whether literary or political, can be settled peaceably. But better than any definition is an example. During the Civil War, Walt Whitman spent three years visiting wounded soldiers in hospitals in and near Washington, D.C. He brought gifts to the patients, ministered to them, talked with them, listened. In his new book *The Dharma of Poetry*, the poet John Brehm writes:

> Among the many remarkable aspects of Whitman's wartime service, perhaps most remarkable is this willingness to tend to Confederate as well as Union soldiers, even though his own brother had been wounded at Fredericksburg, and would later nearly die of starvation in a Confederate prison. Whitman's compassion made no distinctions, and that generosity of spirit informs one of his great short lyrics about the war, published in 1865, after the fighting had ended.

Brehm follows with a brief Whitman poem that sublimely illustrates the poet's generosity of soul. The poem is "Reconciliation":

Word over all, beautiful as the sky!
Beautiful that war, and all its deeds of carnage, must in time be
　　utterly lost;

That the hands of the sisters Death and Night, incessantly softly wash
        again, and ever again, this soil'd world:
For my enemy is dead—a man divine as myself is dead;
I look where he lies, white-faced and still, in the coffin—I draw near;
I bend down, and touch lightly with my lips the white face in the
        coffin.

Tracy K. Smith was born in Falmouth, Massachusetts, in 1972 and was raised in Fairfield, California. She studied at Harvard University, where she joined the Dark Room Collective, a reading series for writers of color. She went on to receive her MFA from Columbia University. Her collection *Life on Mars* (Graywolf Press, 2011) won the 2012 Pulitzer Prize for Poetry. Her other books of poetry are *Wade in the Water* (Graywolf, 2018), winner of the Anisfield-Wolf Book Award; *Duende* (Graywolf, 2007), which was awarded the 2006 James Laughlin Award from the Academy of American Poets; and her debut collection, *The Body's Question* (Graywolf, 2003), which received the Cave Canem Poetry Prize. She is also the author of a memoir, *Ordinary Light*; the editor of an anthology, *American Journal: Fifty Poems for Our Time* (2018), and the cotranslator (with Changtai Bi) of *My Name Will Grow Wide Like a Tree: Selected Poems* by Yi Lei. From 2017 to 2019, she served two terms as the twenty-second Poet Laureate of the United States. She is a Chancellor of the Academy of American Poets.

INTRODUCTION

by Tracy K. Smith

◇　◇　◇

My twelfth-grade history teacher resorted to explaining whole historical movements and value systems by way of the phrase, "It was the spirit of the times." Slavery, Manifest Destiny, Jim Crow. These things weren't born out of deliberate schemes; they simply drifted in on the wind of a unanimous and undeniable zeitgeist.

Sitting in that classroom, or puzzling over lecture notes at home, I had little to no sense of the fears, desires, and deceptions that had set the enterprise of empire into motion. I followed the tableau of American history like a latecomer to a movie-in-progress, longing to know the answers to countless *whys* and *hows*, but dutifully accepting that those explanations were beyond my or anyone's reach.

Throughout the tragedies, violations, griefs, and grievances that shaped 2020, it became clear to me why my teacher—and not just him but so many of the authors of history—insisted upon claiming recourse to an escape hatch like "the spirit of the times." Without it, we're not just inheritors of what was set invisibly into motion by forces beyond anyone's control; we're agents of theft, loss, self-interest, injustice, failure, and disregard. That's a lot of responsibility. But accepting it gives us the right to claim credit for the acts of justice and healing that have kept our species from drifting away like ghosts.

It's by now surely cliché to call 2020 "a year like no other," or to describe all the many ways in which it was "unprecedented." But, even from this little bit of hindsight, I'm still floored by the tsunami of upheaval 2020 brought with it. The world entered a pandemic of such enormous magnitude, it outpaced even our experts' most sobering projections. The tragic loss of life we witnessed—lost to COVID-19 and the inequities it exacerbated, lost to brutality and violence—revealed how truly vulnerable all of us are to our fragile social systems. And yet, in this country, we braved that onslaught with a chorus of contradictory voices: *Don't wear a mask. Wear a mask. It will be gone in a few weeks.*

It will linger longer than anyone wants to believe. We must do something to combat systemic racism. Stand back and stand by.

The uncertainty, the sense of what was at risk changing from day to day, the wish to race ahead to the moment where our current worries would be far behind us—all of that was countered by the sense that time itself had come to a standstill. For me, this meant working from home while parenting my young children through the virtual school day. All the hours that had once neatly sequestered these regions of my life from one another slowed, blurred, collapsed into one. Nothing budged. Even so, I understood myself to be lucky, struggling through the seeming standstill of it all in relative safety.

On May 25, 2020, Amy Cooper, a white woman in Central Park, was caught on video making false accusations to a 911 dispatcher about Christian Cooper, a Black birdwatcher who asked her to leash her dog. One of the most insidious mechanisms of American racism—a white woman's false allegation against a Black man—replayed itself over and again before our eyes, like a case study. Only it ended differently. Christian Cooper was not questioned or captured or carried off by a mob. Amy Cooper was caught out in her lie, America's age-old lie. That same day, George Floyd, a Black man in Minneapolis suspected of using a counterfeit $20 bill, was murdered by police officer Derek Chauvin, who knelt on Floyd's neck for more than nine minutes while onlookers begged for mercy and Floyd called out to his own deceased mother. This, too, was captured on video. This, too, held the key to something age-old and quintessentially American. And it kindled uprisings, protests, and calls for racial justice that constituted a movement.

Was the world still at a standstill, through all of this, or had we begun racing forward into a new phase where time, and the very nature of reality, bent to different laws? Is "law" even the right word, in a world where so much that once seemed concrete—like evidence, like fact—had been rendered abstract and malleable, while so much else—like the deaths that same summer of Breonna Taylor, Ahmaud Arbery, Rayshard Brooks, and David McAtee—continued on in unwavering obedience to the brutal pattern of history?

I believe poetry kept me from succumbing to despair in 2020. A version of that sentence might be true in any given year, but the despair of 2020 was different. I understood much of it to be universal, and a not insignificant part of it to be tribal. The universal despair of being vulnerable to a rampant virus, and the tribal despair of being vulnerable to racially motivated attack. The universal despair of knowing something in America is broken, and the tribal despair of seeing how few are motivated to fix it. I am extraordinarily lucky to have felt both forms of this despair to a lesser degree than many, but even that was enough to prompt crises of both hope and trust. But poetry—the best poems of this rough year—courageously named so much of what I felt myself to be witnessing and enduring. The best poems of 2020 also named many different complex emotional realities with clarity, imagination, rigorous music, and recourse to public history and private recollection. The best poems of 2020 reached me as offerings of desperately needed hope and endurance.

Of course they did. Of course the best poetry to emerge during a bitter year sprang from whatever else was indispensable to sustenance, peace of mind, justice, and healing at the time. What, then, are the gifts to emerge from 2020? How did we minister to ourselves? What did we offer one another?

We sought to do right by the living and the lost—the public heroes and victims of a cruel year, and our very own family members, coworkers, and neighbors who remind us that the essential work of justice is up to us, the living, to commit to. We talked to one another. We lifted one another out of isolation. We drew close to the circle of community, even across all manners of distance. We looked out our windows. We contemplated trees. We watched birds. We took stock of the true scale of our lives on the earth. We sought to love ourselves better. We sought to love strangers better. We did the work of democracy. Humbly, earnestly, we pushed the vehicle of history forward, aware of all that is always seeking to haul it back. The seventy-five poems in this volume bear witness to these and other sustaining acts.

The chorus of voices assembled here consoled and quickened me as I lived out my own version of 2020. But they also remind me that every year is many years, each experienced uniquely by all the many people alive within its frame. If my high-school teacher was even partly correct, and there is a spirit animating our time, I hope it is alert, alive, and ever-adapting, like the voices and imaginations that gave birth to the best poems of this unforgettable year. If there is a spirit animating our time, I hope it is built of music, conscience, rigor, resourcefulness, and even rage. I hope, like these poems, it is asking, even now, *Why? How?*

The Pyramid Scheme

◊　◊　◊

When we say you mellowed
we mean you forgot
the old grievances
like a frying pan
on the stove.

Your whip went lax
like skin, like hope
of going home. You ask and ask
what's for lunch
and when.

And what's more
insulting to all the overtime
you did
than a cut-up hot dog
and decaf
in a plastic cup?

Is this how we end up?
Those of us who
come here? By here you meant
America,
not the nursing
home.

The pay down scheme started
the moment you got
off the boat, I want to scream.

Is that too
angry, too
glib? Instead of fry
I tend to steam.

A TV commercial
promises
a new body. That's
impossible,
you laughed. Now
where are my glasses, my teeth?
The nurses here
steal
everything.

from *Green Mountains Review*

Divination

◊　◊　◊

Thasos, Greece

You begin with the bones, their honey-
combed crevasses airy and bloodless,
the marrow gone to dust.

You finger the hollow cranium, imagine
hooking each vertebra into place—threading
together the chain link spine,

hanging the ribs. The teeth,
you think, would be easiest; how they love order
even now, stone-white soldiers

refusing surrender. The unliving beast
would slowly emerge, terrorless and mute,
a mannequin of its former furred and bleating self.

But this is not what drove you
to pause on the path, to cradle femur, tibia, and shard
in your sack of not-skin, to carry death's leftovers

on your back like a too-tired infant.
When you bring the bones down the mountain,
unbury them one by one, you do not want to

build the beast back, or undo
what brought this horned thing to your table.
Rather, you want to understand surrender,

to see with your own eyes what becomes
of the body, this creaky, bone-borne carriage
you will drive through your life to its end, then,

somehow, let go.

from *Orion Magazine*

Some Call It God

◇   ◇   ◇

I choose Rhythm,
the beginning as motion,
black Funk shaping itself
in the time before time,
dark, glorious and nimble as a sperm
sparkling its way into the greatest of grooves,
conjuring worlds from dust and storm and primordial soup.

I accept the Funk as my holy savior,
Funk so high you can't get over it,
so wide you can't get around it,
ubiquitous Funk that envelopes all creatures great and small,
quickens nerve endings and the white-hot
hearts of stars.

I believe in Rhythm rippling each feather on a sparrow's back
and glittering in every grain of sand,
I am faithful to Funk as irresistible twitch, heart skip
and backbone slip,
the whole Funk and nothing but the Funk
sliding electrically into exuberant noise.
I hear the cosmos swinging
in the startled whines of newborns,
the husky blare of tenor horns,
lambs bleating and lions roaring,
a fanfare of tambourines and glory.

This is what I know:
Rhythm resounds as a blessing of the body,

the wonder and hurt of being:
the wet delight of a tongue on a thigh
fear inching icily along a spine
the sudden surging urge to holler
the twinge that tells your knees it's going to rain
the throb of centuries behind and before us

I embrace Rhythm as color and chorus,
the bright orange bloom of connection,
the mahogany lure of succulent loins
the black-and-tan rhapsody of our clasping hands.
I whirl to the beat of the omnipotent Hum;
diastole, systole, automatic,
borderless. Bigger and bigger still:
Bigger than love,
Bigger than desire or adoration.
Bigger than begging and contemplation.
Bigger than wailing and chanting and the slit throats of roosters.
For which praise is useless.
For which gratitude might as well be whispered.
For which motion is meaning enough.

Funk lives in us, begetting light as bright as music
unfolding into dear lovely day
and bushes ablaze in
Rhythm. Until it begins again.

from Poem-a-Day

Benediction

◊ ◊ ◊

God bless the lightning
bolt in my little
brother's hair.
God bless our neighborhood
barber, the patience it takes
to make a man
you've just met
beautiful. God bless
every beautiful thing
called monstrous
since the dawn
of a colonizer's time.
God bless the arms
of the mother
on the cross
-town bus, the sterling silver
cross at the crux
of her collar bone, its shine
barely visible beneath
her nightshade
navy, New York
Yankees hoodie.
God bless the baby boy
kept precious
in her embrace.
His wail turning
my entire row
into an opera house.
God bless the vulnerable

ones. How they call us
toward love & its infinite,
unthinkable costs.
God bless the floss.
The flash. The brash
& bare-knuckle brawl
of the South Bronx girls
that raised my mother
to grease knuckles, cut eyes,
get fly as any fugitive dream
on the lam,
on the run
from the Law
as any & all of us are
who dare to wake
& walk in this
skin & you
best believe
God blessed
this skin
The shimmer & slick
of it, the wherewithal
to bear the rage of sisters,
brothers slain & still function
each morning, still
sit at a desk, send
an email, take an order,
dream a world, some heaven
big enough for black life
to flourish, to grow God
bless the *no*, my story
is not for sale
the *no*, this body
belongs to me & the earth
alone the *see*, the thing
about souls
is they by definition
cannot be owned God
bless the beloved flesh
our refusal calls

home God bless the unkillable
interior bless the uprising
bless the rebellion bless
the overflow God
bless everything that survives
the fire

from *Literary Hub*

love poem that ends
at popeyes

◇ ◇ ◇

it's valentine's day & i hear tires on the slick streets
it is raining a slow   steady rain
the kind that makes me saddest because it seems
endless   & even after   the sky   having forgotten
its big-eyed blue   stands aloof   now   distant
while the sun   mumbling from her side   of the bed
settles herself   into   a light   doze
i am thinking   of the meal   i won't have to brave
those streets   clamp-thighed   in a passenger seat   to eat
or the flowers i will not have to accept   awkwardly
because flowers are such   strange gifts   why undress
the ground   just to prove   i am special?
we could go to the botanical   gardens   hold hands
smell the smells that come at me   all at once   in a sneeze
or we could pull over on the highway   run through fields
of bonnets   so buckled   with sky
they look   bruised

why has no one ever loved me that way a bonnet
might engorge itself with blue   so much it is a new
color   unnameable   breathless   my loves   hold
their breaths   calculating   they want me   to look
at the food & the flowers & the tiny golden heart
run through   with a golden thread & say thank you thank you
yes   i am wearing silver but now i will wear
only gold & then they expect me to lie down quickly
as if we're children & the fields are bloated with green & it is may

somewhere   the man who doesn't love me   though i wish
i could say the same   is pacing a supermarket floor
his body   a reflection   in the waxed tile
really he is two men   one flesh man   one floor man
& both are moving in a direction away from me
they are picking out fistfuls of roses   or maybe   tulips
maybe assorted flowers with daffodils
& he knows the woman he really loves will dip her nose
into them like a doe & say   thank you   thank you
& she will kiss him with her tacky lips & for the first time
i am not angry that he might lay her down
& ask if he can do   the things he will do
of course she will say yes that is what   you say
when you love someone   right?
it's what i would say   & this time   not
because i've learned what happens
when you say no or when you say   nothing   at all

i am not sad about   whatever she will let him   do
or what she will do to him to make him   smile
make his mouth   form   & his breath catch the emptiness
where a few of his teeth used to be   & make it ache
it's a good ache   when something is missing   & people still love you
i want him to be satisfied   i want him to be happy
also   i want   to be happy   we can do that separately
or we can do it   together   we can do it now
or we can do it   later   i am a hopeless
romantic   i still make wishes before i blow out candles
last week i asked an oracle   when   not if
i'd find true love   it said *bad reception*   *try*
again girl   & i am trying   i am lying
in bed with my arms around   myself   thinking of what
i will eat when i get hungry   i am willing
to wait for what i want   like when i pull up
to the window & the cashier says it'll take ten minutes
for the spicy dark   & i say yeah yeah that's ok
i still want it   & i pull my car over & i play
my music & i imagine the fried flecks of flour
smothering in the saliva   of my mouth

& oh the biscuits & oh the honey & oh the red beans
in their salty velvet   & i think   this is my own gold
it is not   daffodil gold   it is not supermarket-roses-
gold   it is not a thin-   stringed gold attached to a locket
of expectations   with my face clasped between
two   composite   hearts

but it is good   & it is filling   & it is enough

from *The Kenyon Review*

Further Exercises

◇   ◇   ◇

Write a 12-line rhythmically charged poem in which you slant rhyme (at least twice) the name of the last official indicted from the Trump administration. Reference the most recent climate-change related disaster. Address by first name one of the 24 migrants who have died in ICE custody since 2017. End with the instructions given to you by a parent or guardian on what you should do when waking from a nightmare.

★

Write a poem as an acrostic of the name of a person you love who is most vulnerable to US government policies. Include a quote (unattributed) from a writer killed by an authoritarian regime

or a line in which you complete the phrase: "I have birthed _____ and buried _____."

End with a line that snaps like a turnstile at your back, that closes like an iron gate behind you.

★

Typographically represent the 650 miles of border wall teetering on the 2000-mile US–Mexico boundary. Write a 3-word refrain that could be used as a chant to tear the shroud of normalcy. Answer the question: What brought your parents to the place they birthed you? End with a line so open it would allow both a child and an endangered Mexican gray wolf to step through.

*

Begin with the city from which you write. Use your five senses to describe the most recently gentrified neighborhood. Personify a "For Sale" sign or an underfunded public school. Do not include an image of a transient.

*

Write a 48-line poem in which each line ends with you claiming "executive privilege" or some variation of that phrase. Answer the question: What do you call someone who cannot speak and comes without a name? Reference the last time you were terrified by a cop.

End with a metaphor that gasps for air or water

or end with a couplet that screeches like a line drawn in the dirt.

*

Write a poem that binds you and your reader as tightly as the zip ties encircling protestors' wrists. Use empathy, compassion, complicity. Include all the reasons why you have not placed your body in the streets or the courts to protect the person you love who is most vulnerable to the state. Address that person. End with a line that moans like gas entering your tank or end with a line that divides nothing.

*

In couplets, describe the opening shot of a movie you would make to depict the events of the past year. Slant rhyme the name of at least one known Russian hacking virus. Describe a monument, then deface it.

End by completing the phrase: I would _____ 2000 miles to end _____.

*

Write a poem that records all the new developments that have occurred in our country's continued assault on migrants and/or other nonwhite bodies while you were writing any one of the above poems.

★

Make a list of words that sound like shots being fired on a residential street or that sound like children being herded into cages. Create a poem around these words. It should not rhyme.

from *The Brooklyn Rail*

Work

◇ ◇ ◇

—*Romare Bearden*

The men come in every color of black
From the fields of the South
To the mills in the North
And the women too
Some on their feet ready to hoe
Some flat on their backs
One lying facedown
With the train we can trust
In earshot but too far to catch
Very few of us seated
Each so different
You can't tell us apart
The way the skin on my hands
Is not the skin on my face
My face won't get a callus
My hands never had a whitehead
But it's all my body
My body of work is proof
Of color everywhere
I can show you
Just how black everything is
If you let me
If you pay me
If you give me time
To cut
The way a life can be cut into
It's roosters and whistles and sundowns

And other signals to get up
And go to work
Or to rest a little
My family made a little money
And I was so light
A few of the women called me
Shine
I had an eye
For where I wasn't like the people
I pulled and pasted together
Where wasn't I like the people I pasted
Back when Jim Crow touched the black side
Of all the light in the world
First time I came to Atlanta
I couldn't walk through one door
Of the High Museum
Wasn't allowed
But baby I'm old
Enough to know
What New Negro means
Let a Negro show you
Let me do my thing
I want to go to work
I want to make me
Out of us
Turn on the sun
Get me some scissors

from *The Art Section*

After Tu Fu

◇　◇　◇

Soon now, in the winter dawn, I'll face
my 70th year. In the moment it takes

another leaf to fall, I see how many more
evenings I'm going to need sitting here—

letting the wind pass through my hands,
overlooking the star pines and jacarandas,

the valley of home. I think of friends
from my youth, the clear green hills and sea

that traveled with me all this way, all,
almost gone now, despite the longstanding

optimism in stars. A haze drifts between here
and the islands . . . I'm still not sure. . . .

I take an early drink and praise whatever
is left . . . from 10,000 miles away

the wind comes, and the evening air lifts
the atoms of light. One thin cloud, shaped

perhaps like a soul, is back-lit, briefly,
by a rising moon. I stare off wondering

if something more than the resin of pines
will rise on the invisible salt breeze?

What more could I want now beyond
everything I've ever had, all over again,

and the strength to withstand the heavens?
I fold my poems into small paper boats

and send them down the night river . . .
who knows, really, if life goes anywhere?

from *Five Points*

Marfa, Texas

◊   ◊   ◊

Today I tried to open the river.
But when I pulled, the whole
river disappeared. I used to
think that language came from
the body.

Now I know it is in that group
of mountains in the field
beyond the fence. Yesterday, I
saw a red-tailed hawk. When I
went near it, it took

the wind with it. I was left
without air. But I could still
breathe. I realized everything
around me I could do without. I
could hear the

mountains but nothing else. I
saw a car start up but I heard
nothing. A gray-haired woman
said *hello* to me but I heard
nothing. I stood and

watched the hawk. It never
looked at me but knew I was
there. Neither of us moved.
Finally, it flew to the top of an
electric pole.

I realized the pole is all the
years of my life, the mountains'
applause, the hawk, what I have
been trying to tell myself.

from *New England Review*

The School of Eternities

◊　◊　◊

Do you remember the two types of eternity, how we learned
about them in a Wegmans parking lot, when you turned

on the radio, the classical channel? Why
were they even talking about eternity, what

did it have to do with the suddenly
broody guitars? You had a peach

Snapple, I remember the snappy kissy sound of the lid
coming off in your hand. *One type of eternity*, they said, *is inside*

of time, as endless time—life
without death. We were inside our Toyota. I said, *We need*

a new umbrella. Do you remember
when we first rhymed? Do you remember the first time I asked

you about the rain, the expression,
"It's raining cats & dogs," whether it was equally cats & dogs,

falling? Can you remember when you learned the word
"immortality"? The hosts on the classical channel

were okay, I thought you'd do a much better job. I remember saying
so, while you drove us home. Our apartment, our

third. Remember the day we moved
into our first? The boxes of books & boxes of

books? My books? Our sweating up three flights of the greenest
stairs? & you said, *Never again?* & the again, & again,

&? *The other type of eternity is outside of time, beyond it,*
no beginning, no end. I remember. Your hand, the lid, your hands,

the steering wheel, your lips, your lips. The way you took a sip,
gave me a kiss, before starting

to drive.

Do you remember the first time you drove
me home, before "home" meant where we both lived, the books

on the shelves, the books in the closet
when I ran out of shelves, the second apartment, West

Texas, remember the dust, the flat, another type of eternity, that dusty
sun? & driving

to the supermarket, what was it called
there? & that hand soap we'd get, which scent

was your favorite? I don't remember what it was called, can't
remember exactly the smell,

but your hands, after washing, I remember
kissing them. Don't you remember when we thought

only some things were ephemera?
Can you remember when you learned the word

"ephemera," the word "immortality"? Probably the latter
first, & isn't that something,

immortality first, then menus
& movie tickets. What was the first nickname, the fifth

umbrella, the type of taco you ordered on our sixteenth
trip, remember driving, remember when we thought the world

of the world, remember how I signed the letter
explodingly yours, do you remember you were

driving, we were halfway home, only eight minutes
from Wegmans, remember when we measured distance

in terms of Wegmans, like it was a lighthouse
or pyramid or sacred tree, remember when your name

was Fluttersaurus Vex & mine
wasn't, remember when I lived like a letter, falling

in cartoonish slow-mo down four flights of stairs, did you picture
a letter of the alphabet or a letter I'd written

to you, remember when I asked you about the rain, when
the wizard jumped out, when I lied & you laughed, when I lied

& I lied & I lied, can you remember
last night, how I crossed my arms

as though dead & arranged just so, how I pictured my face
polished, as though alive, &

no, you can't remember
that, since it happened while you were sleeping & I

wasn't, I was up, wondering why people always talk about death
as sleep, & how much I love sleep, hate death,

& have I told you about the student who said, *I'm really,*
really afraid of death, just like that,

in class, it was fitting, because it was poetry
class, ha ha, & I loved it, her saying that, I wanted to say I loved it,

but couldn't, I was thinking about you sleeping
& me not, about me sleeping

& you not, & what even is outside of time, beyond
then, now, no

thanks, I'd prefer the type of eternity where we
are inside, are

us, & last night's movie good,
not great, a stray piece of popcorn still under

our coffee table.

Do you remember when the world
signed the letter *yours ephemerally*?

Remember when I asked you about the rain,
the cats & dogs of it,

if it was 50% cats, 50% dogs, 100%
falling, & you said, *Of course*?

& you said, *She's gotten, the flight's not till, I'm going
to drive*. I remember you

driving to your mother, West Texas
to Upstate New York, you didn't make it in time, she had little time,

then none. I remember your face pressed
into my shoulder. I remember your mother was an endless,

a question your face asked into my shoulder. How I wanted it
to answer because I couldn't. I didn't go

with you, when I could've, I chose a poetry reading
instead, thought, she'll be there, you'll be, is memory the best

eternity we can make?
The only?

& you said it's equal, the cats & dogs raining
down, though in terms of overall

volume. The rain, it's all the different breeds of cat, of dog, & see,
there are more individual cats, since there are more

very large breeds of dog,
the cats have to balance things out

with their number, but the dogs, don't you worry, they're raining
down, too, & they're rain,

absolutely, they're still rain, the cats & dogs,
lots of water for the plants, for the flowers, for the whole street

& our dusty car windows, for the cats & dogs
on the ground, the cats & dogs

that aren't rain, at least
not yet, & maybe that's another

eternity, the rainy type.

I remember you drove us home.
The radio was on. We made a sound like a lid coming off.

from *Ploughshares*

Abecedarian for ESL in West Lafayette, Indiana

◇　◇　◇

A is for apples shipped fresh off the
Boat. At 2 PM we left math to go where
Children are taught
Differences between
English and English at home.
For example, Sun-Ah who named herself Sunny
Grabbed blue pills from a plastic bag,
Held the medicine in her palm. Teachers called me in—
Ibuprofen, I say. I am seven,
Just learned the word because Sunny sputtered
Korean that they're painkillers.
Look, English was my second language but
My tongue was new.
Never had to teach me to curl my *R*s
Or how to say *girl*, *blueberries*, *raspberries*. In second grade, I
Played Peter Rabbit's mother rabbit, still don't
Quite know how that happened or
Remember what my lines were.
Still, when the Chicago Field Museum unveiled Sue
The T-Rex, I was Sue the dinosaur, before that, Sue who lived in an old shoe.
Usually I said "Yes, like the T-Rex without the useless *e* at the end."
Versions of my selves in ESL exist but I was kept there, after proficiency.
Who else could translate for the teachers, my parents, and Sunny's parents?
X was for xylophones, x-rays, and now xenophobia.

Yes, that's too on the nose, but things on your nose are hardest to see.
Z is for a zero, zigzagging between classrooms to say she has a fever, she misses home.

from *New England Review*

After the Apocalypse

◊   ◊   ◊

1.

After the apocalypse, I yearned to be reckless. To smash
a glass brought first to my lips. To privilege lust over
tomorrow. To walk naked down the middle of a two-lane
road. But, too late, without my bidding, life cracked open,
rushed, openmouthed, like a panting dog whose name
I did not call—my lips shut like a purse. The last man
I kissed was different than the last man I fucked.
We were so desperate then, the two of us, undone
by longing, drawing night from the cracks
inside us, drawing the night out, as long as we could,
until dawn broke like a beat egg and our heartbeats
quieted in private fatigue. I'd be lying if I said I don't recall
his name. The end of the world has ended, and desire is still
all I crave. Oh, to be a stone, sexless and impenetrable.
Over half of me is water, a river spilling into restless limbs,
the rest of me is a scalding heat like the asphalt under my feet.

2.

After the apocalypse, I mothered my mother, became
grandmother to myself, distant and tender, temples turning
gray. The whole world cascaded past my shoulders, like the hair
self-hatred taught me to crave—though all my Barbie dolls
were black. And the Cabbage Patch Kid my grandmother
placed under the artificial Christmas tree, sprinkled with tinsel,
in Memphis, Tennessee, the city where my mother waited

for her first pair of glasses in the Colored Only waiting room.
She said the world changed from black-and-white to Technicolor
that day. My mother watches TV as I roll her hair. She sits
between my legs. I've never birthed a child. I have fondled the crown
of a lover's head, my thighs framing his dark brown eyes.
I entered the world excised from my mother's womb. Her scar
is a mark the color of time. I am my mother's weeping
wound. On my last birthday, I cried into bathwater.
I hid my tears from my mother because that's what mothers do.

3.

After the apocalypse, I had the urge to dance on the president's
grave. The dispossessed threw me a belated quinceañera. My godmother
wore a necklace of the dictator's teeth. She sliced an upside-down cake,
licked her forefinger, and said, "You have mastered sadness, querida,
may your rage be sticky and sweet." My father offered his hand—this time
I took it. We glided like ballroom dancers across the red dirt floor.
He wore a grave expression. I embraced him tightly
so as to cloak my face. Instead of a toast, he handed me a handkerchief,
wet with tears. My father circled the guests silently, dabbing gently
each of their cheeks. This too was a dance unfolding.
I folded the handkerchief into a fist and raised my fist like
a glass of champagne. The pain in my father's eyes sparkled
like the sequins on my tattered gown. If it hadn't been so ugly
it would've been beautiful. The party ended just as the world had:
with the sound of rain beating against the earth and each of us
on our hands and knees peering into pools of mud and thirst.

4.

After the apocalypse, time turned like a mood ring. My mood
changed like a thunderstruck sky. The sky changed
like a breast, engorged, staining the front of a white silk blouse.
I got laid off. I went thirteen days without wearing a bra. I changed
my mind about the fiction of money. Money changed hands.
I washed my hands religiously. Religion changed into sunlight—
something allowed to touch my face. My face changed into

my mother's. No, into a mask of my mother's face. Traces
of heartache changed into a pain in my right hip. The stock market
dipped. The S&P fell freely. I did not fall to my knees
promising to change my life. The price of paper towels changed
and the price of toilet paper and the price of white bread and milk.
Whiteness did not change. Some things stayed the same. We named
the moon for its changes, but it remained the same. Gravity
pulled at my organs like the moon's tug makes a king tide.
America's king would inevitably change and inevitably stay the same.

5.

After the laughter subsided the crying kept after we held hands
and screamed and screamed and squeezed and screamed after
regret and shame and a single bush filled with speckled thrushes
singing redwing bluebird wood thrush on the wood of a branch
and forest thrush in the branches of a forest open pine
and after your mother refused to haunt your dreams after
you placed her in a wooden coffin and you sang like a blue bird
breast trembling beak open like a mother's beak foraging feeding
offspring after lying on a clutch of blue eggs and after spring
after pining for spring ignorant of your grief and unraveling
with or without your blessing cool days and rain after icicles
crying and after you kept from crying and after you cried
there was no one left to protect after you blessed the demon
possessing you and after it left you were even more alone
a grandala calling and calling and after calling after your mother
a hole closed and a hole opened after that after all of that.

6.

There is a scar near my right eye no lover ever noticed
or kissed, a faint mark: split skin sewn.
And so, and now, there was never a *before*. Never
a time when the wind did not smell of dust
or storm or brine or blood. Never an hour when I entered
a field of bluebells without trampling at least one flower.
And so, and then, on the day I was born, a stampede

of horses filled my chest. Astronomers can only guess
how the universe formed. The planet is dying:
the horses, the mothers, the farmers, the bees. I am
the ground, its many grasses and wild clover.
My teeth grow yellow, ache, decay. I wash a plate,
polishing the moon's face—both will outlast my brutal
hands. And so, in the minutes of *after*, the moon drips
on a silver rack and the plate floats, cracked with age,
in outer space . . . a stray soapsud sparkles then bursts.

from *The Yale Review*

Gross National Unhappiness

◇　◇　◇

No, I am not afraid of you

descending the long white marble steps

from a White Hawk helicopter

to a state-sponsored spectacle

of mansplaining and lies.

If you divide the sea,

you will wind up in a ditch.

The she-goat will mount the he-goat.

Good deeds will cut out our tongues.

No tree will penetrate a radiant sky.

Can't you see our tents cannot be separated?

Can't you see your one thousand dogs

are not greater than our

one thousand gazelles?

from *The American Scholar*

On the Deaths of Friends

◇ ◇ ◇

Either they just die
or they get sick and die of the sickness
or they get sick, recover, then die of something else,
or they get sick, appear to recover
then die of the same thing,
the sickness coming back
to take another bite out of you
in the forest of your final hours.

And there are other ways,
which will not be considered here.
In the evening, I closed my eyes
by the shore of a lake and I pretended
this is what it will look like
or will not look like,
this is where my friends keep going,
a "place" only in quotations marks,

where instead of oxygen, there is silence
unbroken by the bark of a fox in winter
or the whistle of an unattended kettle.
With eyes still closed,
I ran in the dark toward that silence,
like a man running along a train platform,
and when I opened my eyes to see
who was running in the other direction

with outspread arms,
there was the lake again with its ripples,

a breeze coming off the water,
and a low train whistle,
and there was I trembling
under the trees, passing clouds,
and everything else that was pouring
over the mighty floodgates of the senses.

from *The Paris Review*

Interstate Highway System

◊   ◊   ◊

In the beginning, I was
incorporate, plain as skull,

in cahoots though inchoate:
a suit suited to combust—

my body a blunderbuss
brandished in traffic bright

as dogbite. I drifted like sand
under the wind's hand, saw

supercells & speed traps,
saw God in the face of a forest

fire. The sky was froth,
the land foment: ichor & ozone,

bee swarm & wildflower—
every living thing shivering

under the long-range bellow
of the transnational semi-trailer truck.

Thrush melodies tumbled forth
from trees still full of the didactic

temper of birds, but I could only
froth & foment—my tongue

diabetic with word, deeded
as property in the gun safe

of my mouth. Thereafter,
I heeded hints & omens, held

hearsay dear as a family Bible
so listened smartly when gossip

hopscotched households
like housefire. In later years

I leaned prophetic, suffered
visions—saw myself sullen

on a windswept prairie, saw
myself salved in a station flush

with tropical disease, snakes
shaking in my fists like bad mail.

Still, when I slept I slept sound
under the promise of diesel.

When I dreamt I dreamt darkly
under the auspices of convenience.

When I woke I ate in the assurance
of eating all I could. And when

finally I corrected my iconography
I wept to find my eyes ever-blue,

the sun fled—clouds militant,
the moon an ambulance of rock.

Under its urgency I succumbed
to the hobby of my body, held

my health like a cigarette from
the world I watched through

drawn curtains, listening all night
to the opera of wolves behind

the motels of America. Wolves
I ran with, wolves I ran from.

I lived on stick. I lived on stone.
I hunted myself any way I could.

from *The Believer*

Before the Riot

◇　◇　◇

But someone will 'ave to pay
For all the innocent blood . . .
—Bob Marley, "We and Dem"

On the dreary trudge—the frontier begins. A hundred years later,
almost two, a woman says in the way of appeasement,
"Perhaps it is true, that for us to live so well,
some of them had to die. . . ?" The question suggested
by the nervous lift in inflection at the end of phrase—
and who is this "us" who have lived so well, who are living
so well; and how well—so that there is a peculiar
justification, a terrible logic, and it is a haunting
confession buried deep inside the book, though, in truth,
there is no question there. This is its own duplicity, this questioning,
this effortless way of speaking the tragic: there has been blood,
so much blood, and the rituals of bludgeoning,
of rust-tanned white men, clichéd westerners, hunters,
the stereotypes, the killers of vermin rabbits
under-wheel of trucks, the people she knows intimately,
like a daughter knows her father, knows her brothers,
knows the scent of Scotch on her grandfather's breath;
the comfort of their manliness, stoic as stone, they will kill,
as easily as threaten even the softer bodies of their women—
it is a logical equation, a management of ethics,
and who are the dead, the slaughtered and the erased?
Tribes and tribes, whose faces I do not know,
though I know that the logic of this pragmatism—
this expiation of guilt, but the embrace of guilt,
as a kind of penance—is familiar, and the faces of those

bloodshot eyes, skins chalky with deprivation, the weary look
of slaves, those faces are as familiar as the panting bodies
of the football team strewn on the wide grass, undressed
in the heat, sweating, bodies broken after pleasure—the familiar look
of black bodies coffered by desire and violence, familiar as this.
And that saying—that Darwinian logic: "Perhaps it is true,
that for us to live so well, some of them had to die. . . ?"
offered in the soft voice of a Midwestern woman,
who never rushes her words, who carries in her throat
the secret to receiving mercy, a kind of forgiveness,
an expiation of guilt, who we count among those
in whose mouths ice couldn't melt; mouths of tender
duplicity—perhaps, perhaps for us to live
as we do, and by this, I mean we who contemplate
anger and bombs, and chants, today—perhaps,
it's true: that someone will have to pay, as we say.

from *World Literature Today*

The Great Beauty

◊   ◊   ◊

In the movie, flamingos migrate over Rome and rest
overnight on the terrace of Jep Gambardella, so that,

in the rose light of dawn, he walks out to find his saintly
old guest, Sister Maria, meditating amongst a flamboyance—

a hundred stand on pink stilt-like legs with roseate plumes
and beaks sturdy as lobster crackers. Some rest on one leg

or sit with legs tucked under them; some halfheartedly peck
at stone—as if they might find breadcrumbs from last night's party.

But all are quiet. "I know all their Christian names,"
she brags under her breath to no one, or perhaps to God.

★

I never received such tidings from the universe, but Saturday
on my walk, checking my Fitbit again (3000 for an old lady is good) I heard wing beats
and cooing, and then, almost under my arm, one flew up

nearly brushing my hand—as if intentional—then twenty, thirty coming
from behind, as if they were pouring out of my back. I couldn't tell how

many would arrive, a hundred resting on the branches of a tree, and some flying up to a
balustrade, sitting in a long row stolid as judges. Why can't I

take evidence seriously? I (who half believe in God) spoke playfully—
not even remembering I had watched Sister Maria's flamingos two nights

before—"What are YOU doing here?" as if they were old friends or a bunch
of my kids showing up out of nowhere. I watched for a while and when they

just sat there, turning their heads, I went on with my walk—another 1500
steps to go. By the time I was almost home, I had persuaded myself: they're

only pigeons; perhaps hungry. But then they came back, from all around,
as if they were rising up out of the ground, as if they were being made

right before me, all the sounding wings, air whipping and breaking,
their grey and pink presences as if convincing me.

from *The New Yorker*

A Child's Guide to Grasses

◇   ◇   ◇

Or I guess it is a uniform hieroglyphic
—Walt Whitman

Although the smell of fresh-cut grass
is the same everywhere to me

it will always be Hanover:
rec soccer, someone's tamed

plot of land neat and tractored
within a thicket, summer,

its black flies. I sat in grass
on bright secluded days and thought

nothing of the privileged fold
in which I grew. New England's

strange descendants, academics
in the wilderness, proud, protected, civilizing

certain verdure into quads. College
towns are also settlements

of the mind: they trim the world
away. Already there was much

language rooted here I could not
understand. On sunny days I pulled

it up aggressively, a child-sign
for boredom. I am still

most at home on a campus,
which means *field* of course:

as if land naturally
conforms to strategies to turn

the pagan thing into some white
universal. These specific Americas,

selecting certain roots, opulent
with sudden green containment. *Fescue*

more precisely the species that
grew up around me, but

this word harkens to a rod or whip
in Latin, the rigidity we hold when

we hold the land in check. I was
a weak boy. I played alone, would not

proceed into the scrum or run
my kicks in for the ball. The action

seemed unsavory. I had my mud
enough. In school I knew better

how to contain myself. The mind,
too, can colonize its field

color green. I still can taste that full
scent fanned out against a morning,

mowed and mounded, dotting
lawns, spilling onto curbs

like roadkill. Fescue: in English
the word goes back to Wycliffe,

in his version of the Sermon
on the Mount, which warns to note

not the mote in the eye of your brother
before the beam that blinds your own.

from *New England Review*

lake-loop

◊ ◊ ◊

, because there was yet no lake

into many nights we made the lake
        a labor, and its necessary laborings
to find the basin not yet opened
in my body, yet my body—any body
wet or water from the start, to fill a clay
, start being what it ever means, a beginning—
the earth's first hand on a vision-quest
wildering night's skin fields, for touch
        like a dark horse made of air
, turned downward in the dusk, opaquing
a hand resembles its ancestors—
the war, or the horse who war made
        , what it means to be made
to be ruined before becoming—rift
        glacial, ablation and breaking
lake-hip sloping, fluvial, then spilled—

I unzip the lake, walk into what I am—
        the thermocline, and oxygen
, as is with kills, rivers, seas, the water
        is of our own naming
I am wet we call it because it is
a happening, is happening now

imagined light is light's imagination
a lake shape of it
        , the obligatory body, its dark burning

reminding us back, memory as filter
desire as lagan, a hydrology—
     The lake is alone, we say in Mojave

, every story happens because someone's mouth,
a nature dependent—life, universe
     Here at the lake, say
, she wanted what she said
     to slip down into it
for which a good lake will rise—*Lake*
which once meant, *sacrifice*
which once meant, *I am devoted*

     , *Here I am, atmosphere*
sensation, pressure
, the lake is beneath me, pleasure bounded
a slip space between touch and not
slip of paper, slip of hand
     slip body turning toward slip trouble
, I am who slipped the moorings
     I am so red with lack

to loop-knot
or leave the loop beyond the knot
     we won't say love because it is
a difference between vertex and vertices—
the number of surfaces we break
enough or many to make the lake
     loosened from the rock
one body's dearth is another body's ache
     lay it to the earth

, all great lakes are meant to take
     sediment, leg, wrist, wrist, the ear
let down and wct with stars, dock lights
distant but wanted deep,
     to be held in the well of the eye
woven like water, through itself, in
and inside, how to sate a depression
if not with darkness—if darkness is not

fingers brushing a body, shhhh
, she said, I don't know what the world is

I slip for her, or anything
, like language, new each time
        diffusion—remade and organized
and because nothing is enough, *waves—*
each an emotional museum of water

left light trembles a lake figure on loop
        a night-loop
, every story is a story of water
        before it is gold and alone
before it is black like a rat snake
I begin at the lake
, clean once, now drained
        I am murk—I am not clean
everything has already happened
always the lake is just up ahead in the poem
, my mouth is the moon, *I bring it down*
lay it over the lake of her thighs
        warm lamping ax
hewing water's tender shell
slant slip, entering like light, surrounded
into another skin
        where there was yet no lake
yet we made it, make it still
to drink and clean ourselves on

from Poem-a-Day

Love

◇   ◇   ◇

I love you early in the morning and it's difficult to love you.

I love the January sky and knowing it will change although unlike us.

I love watching people read.

I love photo booths.

I love midnight.

I love writing letters and this is my letter. To the world that never wrote to me.

I love snow and briefly.

I love the first minutes in a warm room after stepping out of the cold.

I love my twenties and want them back every day.

I love time.

I love people.

I love people and my time away from them the most.

I love the part of my desk that's darkened by my elbows.

I love feeling nothing but relief during the chorus of a song.

I love space.

I love every planet.

I love the big unknowns but need to know who called or wrote, who's coming—if they want the same things I do, if they want much less.

I love not loving Valentine's Day.

I love how February is the shortest month.

I love that Barack Obama was president.

I love the quick, charged time between two people smoking a cigarette outside a bar.

I love everyone on Friday night.

I love New York City.

I love New York City a lot.

I love that day in childhood when I thought I was someone else.

I love wondering how animals perceive our daily failures.

I love the lines in *Cat on a Hot Tin Roof* when Brick's father says, "Life is important. There's nothing else to hold onto."

I love Brick.

I love that we can fail at love and continue to live.

I love writing this and not knowing what I'll love next.

I love looking at paintings and being reminded I am alive.

I love Turner's paintings and the sublime.

I love the coming of spring even in the most withholding March.

I love skipping anything casual—"hi, how are you, it's been forever"—and getting straight to the center of pain. Or happiness.

I love opening a window in a room.

I love the feeling of possibility by the end of the first cup of coffee.

I love hearing anyone listen to Nina Simone.

I love Nina Simone.

I love how we can choose our own families.

I love when no one knows where I am but feel terrified to be forgotten.

I love Saturdays.

I love that despite our mistakes this will end.

I love how people get on planes to New York and California.

I love the hour after rain and the beginning of the cruelest month.

I love imagining Weldon Kees on a secret island.

I love the beach on a cloudy day.

I love never being disappointed by chocolate.

I love that morning when I was twenty and had just met someone very important (though I didn't know it) and I walked down an almost empty State Street because it was still early and not at all late—and of course I could change everything (though I also didn't know it)—I could find anyone, go anywhere, I wasn't sorry for who I was.

I love the impulse to change.

I love seeing what we do with what we can't change.

I love the moon's independent indifference.

I love walking the same streets as Warhol.

I love what losing something does but I don't love losing it.

I love how the past shifts when there's more.

I love kissing.

I love hailing a cab and going home alone.

I love being surprised by May although it happens every year.

I love closing down anything—a bar, restaurant, party—and that time between late night and dawn when one lamp goes on wherever you are and you know. You know what you know even if it's hard to know it.

I love being a poet.

I love all poets.

I love Jim Morrison for saying, "I'd like to do a song or a piece of music that's just a pure expression of joy, like a celebration of existence, like the coming of spring or the sun rising, just pure unbounded joy. I don't think we've really done that yet."

I love everything I haven't done.

I love looking at someone without need or panic.

I love the quiet of the trees in a new city.

I love how the sky is connected to a part of us that understands something big and knows nothing about it too.

I love the minutes before you're about to see someone you love.

I love any film that delays resolution.

I love being in a cemetery because judgment can't live there.

I love being on a highway in June or anytime at all.

I love magic.

I love the zodiac.

I love all of my past lives.

I love that hour of the party when everyone's settled into their discomfort and someone tells you something really important—in passing—because it's too painful any other way.

I love the last moments before sleep.

I love the promise of summer.

I love going to the theater and seeing who we are.

I love glamour—shamelessly—and all glamour. Which is not needed to live but shows people love life. What else is it there for? Why not ask for more?

I love red shoes.

I love black leather.

I love the grotesque ways in which people eat ice cream—on sidewalks, alone—however they need it, whenever they feel free enough.

I love being in the middle of a novel.

I love how mostly everyone in Jane Austen is looking for love.

I love July and its slowness.

I love the idea of liberation and think about it all the time.

I love imagining a world without money.

I love imagining a life with enough money to write when I want.

I love standing in front of the ocean.

I love that sooner or later we forget even "the important things."

I love how people write in the sand, on buildings, on paper. Their own bodies. Fogged mirrors. Texts they'll draft but never send.

I love silence.

I love owning a velvet cape and not knowing how to cook.

I love that instant when an arc of light passes through a room and I'm reminded that everything really is moving.

I love August and its sadness.

I love Sunday for that too.

I love jumping in a pool and how somewhere on the way up your body relaxes and accepts the shock of the water.

I love Paris for being Paris.

I love Godard's films.

I love any place that makes room for loneliness.

I love how the Universe is 95% dark matter and energy and somewhere in the rest of it there is us.

I love bookstores and the autonomy when I'm in one.

I love that despite my distrust in politics I am able to vote.

I love wherever my friends are.

I love voting though know art and not power is what changes human character.

I love what seems to me the discerning nature of cats.

I love the often-uncomplicated joy of dogs.

I love Robert Lax for living alone.

I love the extra glass of wine happening somewhere, right now.

I love schools and teachers.

I love September and how we see it as a way to begin.

I love knowledge. Even the fatal kind. Even the one without "use value."

I love getting dressed more than getting undressed.

I love mystery.

I love lighting candles.

I love religious spaces though I'm sometimes lost there.

I love the sun for worshipping no one.

I love the sun for showing up every day.

I love the felt order after a morning of errands.

I love walking toward nowhere in particular and the short-lived chance of finding something new.

I love people who smile only when moved to.

I love that a day on Venus lasts longer than a year.

I love Whitman for writing, "the fever of doubtful news, the fitful events; / These come to me days and nights and go from me again, / But they are not the Me myself."

I love October when the veil between worlds is thinnest.

I love how at any moment I could forgive someone from the past.

I love the wind and how we never see it.

I love the performed sincerity in pornography and wonder if its embarrassing transparency is worth adopting in other parts of life.

I love how magnified emotions are at airports.

I love dreams. Conscious and unconscious. Lived and not yet.

I love anyone who risks their life for their ideal one.

I love Marsha P. Johnson and Sylvia Rivera.

I love how people make art even in times of impossible pain.

I love all animals.

I love ghosts.

I love that we continue to invent meaning.

I love the blue hours between three and five when Plath wrote *Ariel*.

I love that despite having one body there are many ways to live.

I love November because I was born there.

I love people who teach children that most holidays are a product of capitalism and have little to do with love—which would never celebrate massacre—which would never care about money or greed.

I love people who've quit their jobs to be artists.

I love you for reading this as opposed to anything else.

I love the nostalgia of the future.

I love that the tallest mountain in our solar system is safe and on Mars.

I love dancing.

I love being in love with the wrong people.

I love that in the fall of 1922 Virginia Woolf wrote, "We have bitten off a large piece of life—but why not? Did I not make out a philosophy some time ago which comes to this—that one must always be on the move?"

I love how athletes believe in the body and know it will fail them.

I love dessert for breakfast.

I love all of the dead.

I love gardens.

I love holding my breath under water.

I love whoever it is untying our shoes.

I love that December is summer in Australia.

I love statues in a downpour.

I love how no matter where on the island, at any hour, there's at least one lit square at the top or bottom of a building in Manhattan.

I love diners.

I love that the stars can't be touched.

I love getting in a car and turning the keys just to hear music.

I love ritual.

I love chance, too.

I love people who have quietly survived being misunderstood yet remain kids.

And yes, I love that Marilyn Monroe requested Judy Garland's "Over the Rainbow" to be played at her funeral. And her casket was lined in champagne satin. And Lee Strasberg ended the eulogy by saying, "I cannot say goodbye. Marilyn never liked goodbyes, but in the peculiar way she had of turning things around so that they faced reality, I will say au revoir."

I love the different ways we have of saying the same thing.

I love anyone who cannot say goodbye.

from *The American Poetry Review*

Naji, 14. Philadelphia.

◇　　◇　　◇

A bench, a sofa, anyplace flat—
just let me down
somewhere quiet, please,
a strange lap, a patch of grass . . .

What a fine cup of misery
I've brought you, Mama—cracked
and hissing with bees.
Is that your hand? Good, I did
good: I swear I didn't yank or glare.

If I rest my cheek on the curb, let it drain . . .

They say we bring it on ourselves
and trauma is what *they* feel
when they rage up flashing
in their spit-shined cars
shouting *Who do you think you are?*
until everybody's hoarse.

I'm better now. Pounding's nearly stopped.

Next time I promise I'll watch my step.
I'll disappear before they can't
unsee me: better gone
than one more drop in a sea of red.

from *The Paris Review*

This'll hurt me more

◊ ◊ ◊

Don't make me send you outside to find a switch,
my grandmother used to say. It was years before
I had the nerve to ask her why switch was the word
her anger reached for when she needed me to act
a different way. Still, when I see some branches—
wispy ones, like willows, like lilacs, like the tan-yellow
forsythia before the brighter yellow buds—I think,
these would make perfect switches for a whipping.
America, there is not a place I can wander inside you
and not feel a little afraid. Did I ever tell you about that
time I was seven, buckled into the backseat of the Volvo,
before buckles were a thing America required.
My parents tried, despite everything, to keep us
safe. It's funny. I remember the brown hills sloping
toward the valley. A soft brown welcome I looked for
other places but found only there and in my grandmother's
skin. Yes, I have just compared my grandmother's body
to my childhood's hills, America. I loved them both,
and they taught me, each, things I needed to learn.
You have witnessed, America, how pleasant hillsides
can quickly catch fire. My grandmother could be like that.
But she protected me, too. There were strawberry fields,
wind guarded in that valley, tarped against the cold.
America, you are good at taking care of what you value.
Those silver-gray tarps made the fields look like a pond
I could skate on. As the policeman questioned my dad,
I concentrated on the view outside the back window.
America, have you ever noticed how well you stretch
the imagination? This was Southern California. I'd lived

there all my life and never even seen a frozen pond.
But there I was, in 70 degree weather, imagining
my skates carving figure eights on a strawberry field.
Of course my father fit the description. The imagination
can accommodate whoever might happen along.
America, if you've seen a hillside quickly catch fire
you have also seen a river freeze over, the surface
looking placid though you know the water deep down,
dark as my father, is pushing and pushing, still trying
to get ahead. We were driving home, my father said.
My wife and my daughters, we were just on our way
home. I know you want to know what happened next,
America. Did my dad make it safely home or not?
Outside this window, lilac blooms show up like a rash
decision the bush makes each spring. I haven't lived
in Southern California for decades. A pond here
killed a child we all knew. For years after that accident,
as spring bloomed and ice thinned, my daughter
remembered the child from her preschool. And now,
it's not so much that she's forgotten. It's more that
it seems she's never known that child as anything other
than drowned. My grandmother didn't have an answer.
A switch is what her mother called it and her grandmother
before her. She'd been gone from that part of America
for over half a century, but still that southern soil
sprang up along the contours of her tongue. America,
I'll tell you this much, I cannot understand this mind,
where it reaches. Even when she was threatening
to beat me, I liked to imagine the swishing sound
a branch would make as it whipped toward my body
through the resisting air. She'd say, this is hurting me
more than it's hurting you. I didn't understand her then,
but now I think I do. America, go find me a switch.

from *Literary Hub*

Stone Love

◇　◇　◇

I spent a star age in flames
Bolted to the black heavens
Waiting for you.

Light crept over the sill of the earth
A thousand upon ten thousand
Upon a hundred thousand years
But no light touched me
Deep in depthless time
Waiting for you.

Fate flung me out,
Hauled me here
To love as a stone loves
Waiting for you.

Touch me, butterfly.
Like you, I have no hands.
Kiss me, rain.

Like you, I have no mouth.
Snow sit heavily upon me.
Like you, I can only wait.

Come to me, dear
Unenduring little
Human animal.

I have no voice
But your voice.
Sing to me. Speak.
Let the clouds fly over us.
I have spent a star age in flames
Just to hold you.

from *Freeman's*

Conqueror

◊   ◊   ◊

The lights are green as far as I can see
all down the street, sweet spot pre-dawn,
a Sunday, no one out. I measure time
in travel now. This route's a favorite, half
derelict, half grand, an oak hydrangea
blooming on old wood. I left a note
in felt tip for my dad, prepped him, then
reminded him last night, but at 4 I had to
mime and mouth for him *Go back to bed*,
my head tilted on sideways prayer hands.
He looked blank, obeyed. The ophthalmologist
explained how hard it is to see behind
his pupils; I forget the reasons why.
I'm at the terminal with the other early flyers,
thinking of the faces of the ancient kings
I've seen, their ears of stone, and their eyes,
no matter the direction or the time, looking,
as we must presume, ahead, and not inside.

from *The Kenyon Review*

They Ran and Flew
from You

◇   ◇   ◇

Your days are ordinary to and from school along the park esplanade.

The children alert as birds and as flitting and as chirping. The sunlight

through the Ficus and jacaranda canopy. The children run and fly

from you to perch on the rainbow half shell egg seats. Children alight

above your head onto the mama bird's yellow-ringed neck. A yellow

clump of wildflowers they pull from the ground and suck the stems.

They warn you not to eat the petals, which are poisonous. Into the red

birdhouse, children chatter and *cor-cori-coo* in echoing loops and

in the echo's end, they call out again. You watch them kaleidoscope

like butterflies. They flap and fight over the lavender and spring yellow

and peach winged seats. You watch the clambering onto the royal blue

musical instruments emerging from the ground; curling into the body

of sound, into the shape of tuba and trombone bells. The children take off their socks and shoes to scale a snail's hump. The reward is a tree

dangling its baubles of pitanga cherries—and adjacent a fence's vines

laden with passionfruit—children rip open the top with their teeth and

slurp out the seeds and neon juice. You watch the children assemble a row

before the national flags and the banners sketched with national songs.

You listen as the children pitch their voices in unison.

from *The Southern Review*

I Feel Good

◇   ◇   ◇

On the occasion of the state of South Carolina taking control of the
$100 million James Brown I Feel Good Trust, willed to the
education of needy students, and after the death of Prince

Whores raised him *with intellect*
and savoir faire, teaching:

pack your fragrant pants proper
like a mattress, stock the edges

for comfort, with newspaper
headlines & purple velvet cock feathers,

scrupulously tilt the tucked
microphone like it's your johnson,

hips travel best when horizontal of how
the crow flies, keep spinning and splendor

in your daily moves, know sound
is gilt-edged & saturnalian like lightning,

meant to enter but never land, cotton-slide
your closed eyes all the way back to Watusi land;

caterwaul & amplify,

exalt yourself on your backside,
spell yourself out with your alligator feet,

the world will prefer you in heels,

when you *open up the door*
sport hot curls and a sexy cape,

drop to your knees before, during, and after
the end of every song,

clothes are tight for a reason,
sweat is money in any season,

men pretending to be wallflowers
are all ears and antsy in the parlor,

straining at the bit
for you to finish your dying.

from *The Atlantic*

Night School

◊   ◊   ◊

I am against
symmetry, he said. He was holding in both hands
an unbalanced piece of wood that had been
very large once, like the limb of a tree:
this was before its second life in the water,
after which, though there was less of it
in terms of mass, there was greater
spiritual density. Driftwood,
he said, confirms my view—this is why it seems
inherently dramatic. To make this point,
he tapped the wood. Rather violently, it seemed,
because a piece broke off.
Movement! he cried. That is the lesson! Look at these paintings,
he said, meaning ours. I have been making art
longer than you have been breathing
and yet my canvases have life, they are drowning
in life—Here he grew silent.
I stood beside my work, which now seemed rigid and lifeless.
We will take our break now, he said.

I stepped outside, for a moment, into the night air.
It was a cold night. The town was on a beach,
near where the wood had been.
I felt I had no future at all.
I had tried and I had failed.
I had mistaken my failures for triumphs.
The phrase *smoke and mirrors* entered my head.
And suddenly my teacher was standing beside me,
smoking a cigarette. He had been smoking for many years,

his skin was full of wrinkles.
You were right, he said, the way
instinctively you stepped aside.
Not many do that, you'll notice.
The work will come, he said. The lines
will emerge from the brush. He paused here
to gaze calmly at the sea in which, now,
all the planets were reflected. The driftwood
is just a show, he said; it entertains the children.
Still, he said, it is rather beautiful, I think,
like those misshapen trees the Chinese grow.
Pun-sai, they're called. And he handed me
the piece of driftwood that had broken off.
Start small, he said. And patted my shoulder.

from *The Threepenny Review*

Tilt-A-Whirl

◇　◇　◇

It was a hot day in Paola, Kansas.
    The rides were banging around empty

as we moved through the carnival music and catcalls.
    At the Tilt-A-Whirl we were the only ones.

My big sister chose our carriage carefully,
    walking a full circle until she stopped.

The ride operator didn't take his eyes off her
    long dark hair and amber eyes, ringed

like the golden interior of a newly felled pine.
    She didn't seem to notice him lingering

as he checked the lap bar and my sister asked
    in her sweetest, most innocent—or maybe

not-so-innocent—voice, *Can we have a long ride*
    please, mister? When he sat back down

at the joystick, he made a show
    of lighting his smoke and the cage

of his face settled into a smile
    I would one day learn to recognize.

Here was a man who knew
    his life would never get better,

and those dizzying red teacups began to spin
      my sister and me into woozy amusement.

We forgot the man, the heat, our thighs
      sticking to the vinyl seats, our bodies glued

together in a centrifugal blur of happiness
      beneath a red metal canopy

as we picked up speed and started to laugh,
      our heads thrown back, mouths open,

the fabric of my sister's shirt clinging
      to the swinging globes of her breasts

as we went faster, and faster,
      though by then we had begun to scream, *Stop!*

Please stop! Until our voices grew hoarse
      beneath the clattering pivots and dips,

the air filling with diesel and cigarettes, and the man
      at the control stick, waiting for us

to spin toward him again, and each time he cocked his hand
      as if sighting prey down the barrel of a gun.

from *New Ohio Review*

I Won't Live Long

◇ ◇ ◇

enough to see any of the new
dreams the hundreds of new kinds of suffering and weeds birds animals shouldering their
demise without possibility of re-
generation the heart in your tiny chest opening its new unimaginable ways of
opening and to what might it still
open. Will there still be
such opening. Will you dare. I will not be there
to surround you w/the past w/my ways of
knowing—to save
you—shall you be saved—from what—
home from fighting are you, remembering how he or she or they looked at you
while you both fed the machine or built the trough in dirt
where it will be necessary to
plant again—will it open—will the earth open—will the seeds that remain—will you know to
find them in
time—will those who have their lock on you
let the openings which are
chance unknowing loneliness the unrelenting arms of
form, which knows not yet the form
it will in the end
be, open and
form? Will there be islands. Will there be a day where you can afford to think back far
enough to the way we loved you. Words you said
for the first time
as we said them. *Mystery* your grandfather said one day, after saying *shhh* listen to the
birds & you sat so still,
all your being arcing out to hear,
and the bird in its hiding place gave us this future, this moment today when you can recall—
can you—his saying, *there,*

that's a mystery.
And you said the word as if it were new ground to stand on,
you uttered it to stand on it—
mystery. Yes, mystery he said. Yes mystery you said
talking to it now as it
took its step out of the shadow into the clearing and there you
saw it in the so-called in-
visible. Then when the wave broke the first time on what had seemed
terra firma and you knew as he held your hand
insisting you hold your ground
that there was foreclosure,
there was oldness of a kind you couldn't fathom, and there was the terrifying
suddenness of the
now. Your mind felt for it. It felt the reach from an elsewhere and a dip which cannot hold.
Splash went the wave.
Your feet stood fast.
Your hem was touched.
We saw you watch.
We felt your hand grip
but not to move back.
Can you find that now now, wherever you are, even a candle would be a gift I know
from there. *Shhh* he said so you could hear it. *Pity* he said
not knowing to whom.
Pity you said, laughing, *pity pity*, and that was the day of
your being carried out
in spite of your cold, wrapped tight, to see the evening star. And he pointed. And you
looked up. And you took a breath I hear even now as I go
out—the inhalation of dark secrecy fear distance the reach into an almost-touching
of silence, of the thing that has no neighbors and never will, in you,
the center of which is noise,
the outermost a freezing you can travel his arm to with your gaze
till it's there. The real. A star. The earth is your
home. No matter what they tell you now and what program you input via your chip or port
or faster yet, no, no, in that now I am not there
in, to point, to take your now large hand and say
look, look through these fronds,
hold your breath,
the deer hiding from the hunter is right here in our field,
it knows we are too,
it does not fear us.

74

Be still. Wait. And we, we
will be left behind.
Except just now. If you still once.
That you might remember.
Now. Remember now.

from *The New Yorker*

Hunger

◇ ◇ ◇

Weeks after her death I came to the garden window
to marvel at sudden pale feathers catching, scattering
past the rainy glass. I looked for magic everywhere.
Signs from the afterlife that I was, indeed, distinct.
Beneath the talon of a red-tailed hawk a pigeon
moved briefly until it didn't. The hawk stripped
the common bird, piercing its thick neck. Beak probing body
until I could see the blood from where I stood inside.
This could happen, naturally enough, even in Brooklyn.
This could happen whether or not my mother was dead.
I didn't eat for weeks because it felt wrong to want bread & milk.
The hawk's face running red, beautiful as it plucked & picked
its silver-white prey apart. It wasn't magic, but hungrily, I watched.
As if I didn't know memory could devour corpses
caught alive in midair. I opened the window,
knelt on the fire escape. I was the prey
& hawk. This was finally myself swallowing
those small, common parts of me. Tearing all of that away
into strips, pulling my breast open to the bone. I saw myself
torn apart, tearing & tearing at the beautiful face,
the throat beneath my claw. My grieving face red
with being exactly what I knew myself to be.

from *The Paris Review*

FRANCINE J. HARRIS

Sonata in F Minor,
K.183: Allegro

◊　◊　◊

[Domenico Scarlatti, Daria van den Bercken]

Car tires rush through and announce the rain. You can hear
the shuffling of someone street sweeping in the street.
The insistent men outside Stingray's, the cutoff lull
of ambulance testing siren, the women. who step in the street and yell
to anyone they loved once and it sounds like prelude if
　　　　Scarlatti hadn't moved to Madrid

　　　　would he have moved the notes diatonically as the rain falls up

a roof. ascends the scaffolding. It's impossible to read *The Street*
without seeing Mrs. Hedges on mine. leaning from a window on the ground
level. of my building peering out under her red bandana considering
me as I lean my body over the railing and watch the men dressed
black and in gray I tell a man to stop peeing on my car and when
　　　　he turns around. he is not surprised. He says

　　　　he isn't peeing, he

is counting his money.

from *The New York Review of Books*

77

George Floyd

◇   ◇   ◇

You can be a bother who dyes
his hair Dennis Rodman blue
in the face of the man kneeling in blue
in the face the music of his wrist-
watch your mouth is little more
than a door being knocked
out of the ring of fire around
the afternoon came evening's bell
of the ball and chain around the neck
of the unarmed brother ground down
to gunpowder dirt can be inhaled
like a puff the magic bullet point
of transformation both kills and fires
the life of the party like it's 1999 bottles
of beer on the wall street people
who sleep in the streets do not sleep
without counting yourself lucky
rabbit's foot of the mountain
lion do not sleep without
making your bed of the river
boat gambling there will be
no stormy weather on the water
bored to death any means of killing
time is on your side of the bed
of the truck transporting Emmett
till the break of day Emmett till
the river runs dry your face

the music of the spheres
Emmett till the end of time

from *The New Yorker*

Waste Management

◇   ◇   ◇

(Skokie, 1970)

Punch the time clock
and try to keep up
with the two collectors
who trained you
since they need to finish
the route in five hours
and get to their second jobs
on time, move steadily
behind the truck,
don't stop to rest
in the shade
between the houses,
don't dawdle or slip
on the gravel
in the alley, watch out
for needles
and broken glass,
it's hot as a dustbowl
in August, but don't wipe
the sweat from your face
with your glove
or your torn sleeve,
lift the trash cans
with your whole body,
don't embarrass yourself
and wave to a girl
from the step

of the garbage truck
racing down Niles Center Road
on the way to the dump
at the end of the day,
don't roll on the carpet
in rage when you get home
or slam the door to your room
and topple the trophies,
never turn yellow-eyed
with hepatitis
and land in the hospital
just to be seen.

from *Five Points*

David

◇   ◇   ◇

You marveled at the vein in the marble.
The moment's slight pulse when you approached.
His blood murmured when you neared, so I
believed, and still do. When I returned to
it, you were gone in the other country
of my head that will never, like him, age.
Long was I able to stare at the vein.
The giant must've just laughed and mocked him.
Then he imagined the giant's fall, and heard
a restless quiet as far as Sokho.
He thought of the river near the vineyard,
its broad dreaming-stone. He knew it no more.
The animals looked inconsolable.
They knew their boy was lost to become king.
I was supposed to photograph you both;
but the stone sank in me and I didn't;
my eyes going between David's and your eyes
as the army, scattered, pushed us apart,
the tumult blotted out what I shouted
to you, which he heard, turned, nodded gently
with a killer's uncommon sympathy.

from *The New York Review of Books*

DIDI JACKSON

Two Mule Deer

◊   ◊   ◊

walked past my window
this morning—female

I think, no antlers,
as the day-moon pressed

like a faded thumbprint
into the bare back

of the Santa Cruz Mountains
and the meadow of wild rye

and wand buckwheat rocked
in the new light,

all hide and eyes and hunger
moving with caution and blaze.

Is there a coming of good?
As if their path was already decided,

I watched them step into the day,
black tail tipped and wide eared.

So much of what I want
isn't even about me.

Yesterday, a friend said
the sight of deer means danger

is clear. No coyote
or mountain lions nearby.

Still, I remember
what it feels like

to be a sidewalk,
a girl suddenly

tamped down
at an all-night party,

fingered then dropped
by a boy who will

be dishonorably discharged
from the Army

only two years later.
You know how it feels

wanting to walk into
the rain and disappear—

While hiking,
a photographer found

two deer legs
about one hundred feet apart.

Cloven hooves and dewclaws
intact. Adapted for fleeing

predators. Left by a hunter.
We are only what we are.

Don't pity me.
A slight steam rises

from the backs of the deer
as they move past

the black oaked edge
into the white light

lifting their eyes
to the tree line,

then to my window,
then to the sky,

hooves striking the ground
over and over

like the syllables
of a low staccato voice.

from *The Kenyon Review*

Double Major

◇   ◇   ◇

I emerge whenever he confuses the lamp for a moon.
It is then he thinks of fine bindings in ordered athenaeums.
I own his face, but he washes and spends too little time behind his ears.
He sees me in the mirror behind thick clouds of shaving
    cream then suddenly believes in ghosts.
His other selves are murals in the cave of his mind. They are speechless
    yet large. They steer his wishes like summer rain and amplify
    his terrors like newscasters.
What he doesn't know: his dreams are his father's dreams, which are his
    grandfather's dreams, and so on. *They* possessed a single wish.
He knocks repeatedly on the bolted door to his imagination.
Tragically, he believes he can mend his wounds with his poetry.
And thus, I am his most loyal critic. He trots me out like a police dog.
He calls our thirst for pads and pencils destiny.
Our voices come together like two wings of a butterfly.
On occasion, he closes his eyes and sees me.
I am negative space: the test to *all men are created equal*.
We are likely to dance at weddings against my will. He pulled out the same
    moves writing this poem, a smooth shimmy and a hop.
This page is a kind of looking glass making strange whatever stone-carvings
    he installed along the narrow road to his interior.
I suffer in silence wedded to his convictions. He would like to tell you
    the truth about love. But we are going to bed, to bed.

from *The Yale Review*

So Much for America

◇   ◇   ◇

I was interrogated via helicopter
while taking a shortcut through
a field I was handcuffed leaving
this post office I was placed in
a lineup in the middle of the street
I dress nattily I wear sports jackets
I use rubbing alcohol to keep
my sneakers clean My sweatshirts
with the stitched block letters
from certain colleges won't stop
complete strangers from searching
my crotch I whisper uncontrollably
I smile when nothing's funny Gun
at my temple Shit stinging my ear
Is that a knife in your hand I thought
protocol was the scruff of your collar
On the curb On your stomach
Cheekbone on the hood The smell
of good wax I'm so aware of my
body Do you think about your body
Look at your hands Show me your
hand I'm returning to Ellison
I'm surrounded You're surrounded
But I'm always alone

from *The Southern Review*

Wheelchair

◇　◇　◇

Weeks on my back, counting
stars not up there, cutting quick
close corners in the wheelchair

Ralph kept moving true as oil,
questions silent in my mouth
after hearing a ragged sound

rattle loose from other souls
as if within my own body,
trying not to drag my foot,

& near misses in the hallway
pumped dares through blood
as we rolled into the elevator.

I can see my great-grandma
Sarah, as wheels of her chair
furrowed those chopped rows,

feet curled under her, a rake
or a hoe held in strong hands,
weeding corn, beans, & potatoes

dug to feed her hungry family
down in the Mississippi Delta,
& today it is not hard to hear

a moan rise out of black earth
where this woman raised hot
red peppers for her turtle soup.

from *The Paris Review*

Immigrant Song

◊ ◊ ◊

Bitter Mother

Blue, dead, rush of mothers,
conceal your island, little star.

Trains, hands, note on a thread,
Poland's dish of salt.

They said, The orphanlands
of America
          promise you a father—

The ship's sorrows, broken daughter,
the ocean's dark, dug out.

Silent Father

Rain, stars, sewage in the spill,
hush the river.

your black boat, broken snake,
you hid. You sailed

for the meritlands of America,
dumped your name in the black
          water—

In the village they pushed the Rabbi
to the wall—someone
        blessed the hunter.

Angry Daughter

One says No and the other
        says nothing at all—

Chicago, I will live in your museums
where Europe is a picture on the wall.

Obedient Child

I concealed my island,
my little star.

In my black boat I hid.
I hid in pictures on the wall.

I said, I am here in America,
your hero, your confusion,

your disappointment after all.
They said,

How did you end up so bad
in a country this good and tall.

from *The Nation*

91

The End of Poetry

◇   ◇   ◇

Enough of osseous and chickadee and sunflower
and snowshoes, maple and seeds, samara and shoot,
enough chiaroscuro, enough of thus and prophecy
and the stoic farmer and faith and our father and tis
of thee, enough of bosom and bud, skin and god
not forgetting and star bodies and frozen birds,
enough of the will to go on and not go on or how
a certain light does a certain thing, enough
of the kneeling and the rising and the looking
inward and the looking up, enough of the gun,
the drama, and the acquaintance's suicide, the long-lost
letter on the dresser, enough of the longing and
the ego and the obliteration of ego, enough
of the mother and the child and the father and the child
and enough of the pointing to the world, weary
and desperate, enough of the brutal and the border,
enough of can you see me, can you hear me, enough
I am human, enough I am alone and I am desperate,
enough of the animal saving me, enough of the high
water, enough sorrow, enough of the air and its ease,
I am asking you to touch me.

from *The New Yorker*

In the Village

◇   ◇   ◇

1.

Shortly before I died,
Or possibly after,
I moved to a small village by the sea.

You'll recognize it, as did I, because I've written
About this village before.
The rocky sliver of land, the little houses where the fishermen once lived—

We had everything we needed: a couple of rooms
Overlooking the harbor,
A small collection of books,
Paperbacks, the pages
Brittle with age.

How, if I'd never seen
The village, had I pictured it so accurately?
How did I know we'd be happy there,
Happier than ever before?

The books reminded me of what,
In our youth,
We called literature.

2.

The sentences I've just written
Took it out of me.
I searched for the words,
And I resisted them as soon as I put them down.

Now, listening to them again, what I hear
Is not so much nostalgia
As a love of beginning. A wish

Never to be removed
From time but
Always to be immersed in it.
The boats come in, the boats go out—

3.

After a routine ultrasound revealed a fifteen-centimeter mass, my left
kidney was removed robotically on February 12th. Fifteen months
later, nodules were discovered in my lungs and peritoneum. Two
subsequent rounds of therapy failed to impede their growth, so I
enrolled in a trial, a treatment not yet FDA approved.

Shrinkage of the tumors was immediate, as was the condensation of
my sense of time: moments in my youth once distant, even irrelevant,
felt burningly present. Didn't everyone, my parents, my grandparents,
grow old before they died? Then what about Tony? What about Russ?
Hadn't their lives, though long past fifty, only begun?

I walked down High Street to the harbor, though when I say *walked* I
mean imagined; I hadn't been there yet.

4.

The Branch Will Not Break.

A Cold Spring.

Leaflets.

The Lost World.

The Moving Target.

Nightmare Begins Responsibility.

Rivers and Mountains.

The Story of Our Lives.

Untitled Subjects.

Water Street.

5.

Of ghosts pursued, forgotten, sought anew—
Everywhere I go
The trees are full of them.

From trees come books, that, when they open,
Lead you to expect a person
On the other side:

One hand having pulled
The doorknob
Towards him, the other

Held out, open,
Beckoning
You forward—

6.

Ash-blond, tall, a sweater
Knotted by its sleeves around his neck,
A boy is leaning on a bicycle. Deftly when she reaches him

A girl slips to the grass, one hand straightening her skirt,
The other tugging at the boy, who remains
Standing, to sit beside her.

Their heads are close
Enough to be touching;
Their lips are still—

A book is the future.
You dream
Of reading it, and once you've finished, it's a miracle, you know the past.

The sky fills with stars. The sun
Climbs every morning
Over Watch Hill, dropping behind the harbor at dusk.

Water Street runs past
Church and Wall,
Harmony and School,
Until it crosses Omega, by the sea.

from *The American Poetry Review*

Meditations on a Photograph of Historic Rail Women

◊   ◊   ◊

Number two from the right was an angry drunk.
Number one from the left always held the face of a dead cousin in her left pocket.
The third woman placed fourth in a seed spitting contest at age six.
The first one knew she was the prettiest.
The fifth didn't need to know.

The child belonging to the one on the far right worked at the general store as a bagboy.
The first's daughter was too rough looking. She lived to be sixty-one.

The second woman had no children. She spent five minutes picking the right shovel. It was as black as her hands. This was not the first time she swung metal things from the waist.

The first woman's head-wrap was a dishrag she grabbed just before leaving.
The second woman's head-wrap was a gift from a long-dead suitor.
The center woman's head-wrap was a prop.

The second from the left quit two days in.
The first preferred to use a wrench.
The center woman got the second to do her work.
The first wouldn't stop for all money in the world.

Right from the center's brother was a saint who shot himself last year.
The fourth girl from the right gave up on God long ago.
The fifth girl was a woman by the time she was thirteen.
The fifth from the other side decided she would never grow up as soon as the papers were signed.

I think the second had money saved but had something to prove.
The fourth looks like a Virgo.
The second woman was raped.
The first woman was raped.
At least three were raped and, during the interview, four said they once knew true love.
A white woman slapped two for being insolent.
The middle lady shot a nigga.
The last woman fondled her cousin when she was young. Is that the same cousin who died?
Is the last woman dead?

My grandmother is eighty-six.
I have no pictures of her, but I do know her name.
Her name is Ruth.
She loves God more than life.
She calls young black men monsters each time I visit. She never leaves the house.
She grew up on a Virginian farm.
She is separated from but on good terms with my granddad.

My granddad's name is Sonny.
My granddad can't read.
He would look hard at the caption for this photo of nameless women and say,

> *I'm sorry, Warren.*
> *I don't have my glasses on me.*
> *Why don't you just tell me what it says?*

from *The American Poetry Review*

When My Sorrow Was Born

◇   ◇   ◇

after Kahlil Gibran

When my Sorrow was born, I held it, a dark pearl spit from its shell, and I remembered the salt that had rounded it before, centuries ago, before I even had a mouth.

And my Sorrow was unafraid and it gave me bravery and my anger back, walked me to the tossing water and proclaimed the water mine.

My Sorrow held me and did not tell me not to cry, and the girls about me watched our sweet days together with longing, for they too wanted to be held by something with fingers as slender and delicate as my Sorrow's, fingers that tapped their temples and had them see how they had been wronged.

And those who longed for my Sorrow would never have a Sorrow like mine. I knew that, for my Sorrow had a forest black mane like mine.

And my Sorrow let me say I, I, mine.

And my Sorrow sat with me on the fire escape all that breathing winter, and my Sorrow would not let me into the water.

And my Sorrow deveined shrimp and patterned them on my plate, brought me a wide bowl brimming with broth.

And we ate fried eggs with chopsticks. We waited for my Joy to come.

from *New Ohio Review*

All the Stops

◇ ◇ ◇

Rolling through the intersection, I see in my rearview
the back of the familiar octagon rusted over, belying
the option of following its forward-facing order.

The driver behind me brakes just as half-heartedly,
and for a moment I pretend together we'd make one
whole heart's best effort to postpone the hurt and hurtle

past the red fur of thorn and bud beyond the shoulders
as the season nips the next one's heels. IF YOU CAN'T
SEE MY MIRRORS I CAN'T SEE YOU warns the sticker

affixed to the glint of the bumper ahead, but I've only got
eyes for the peripheral blood smear shimmer where
whatever winter took is finally kicking in. All those years

wishing I were sure and thin as a sign and could wait
for no mandible nor manager nor manna nor mention.
All those years I told my charges to hold my hand

and look both ways as I told myself to stop at nothing.
Don't let go. Let go. Everywhere, the referents of other
people's safe words—dive bars dropping paint flakes

and first flowers face-down with the sun on their napes.
A tinge of desperation in every command. Take it
from me. Ahead a sky scored by some flight's velocity,

contrail kindred in its substance—water, pressure. Two lights
at a complicated crossing and the capitals cry THIS IS YOUR

SIGNAL. Sure, but there are other shapes in me, flipped
evergreen like rare old color film and just as quick to burn.

from *The Southampton Review*

Playing Dead

◇ ◇ ◇

The first time I was touched,

parts of me were seen:
the nautilus, the teeth,

the cavern of mouth, how a question
marks the spine and then it is never

answered
how his seeing became my seeing

he surprised me his finger
slipped into

a barren—burrows
a bare

contusion
I thought I was exposed

but unbeknownst to me,
most parts remained unseen

and I was to retain this unseen feeling
most of my life
I've spent apart, not a part

of any tribe or religion or posse
most of my life I identified with animals

like the possum
searching for trash or playing dead

After this thing was done to me
I believed I played a part in it

an actress finds a part
so she could slip, finally, into another skin
my parts, these parts

I wrote the whole thing
off, my feelings were leaves
that bypassed everyone and buried me

in autumn, my seams parted
and all I did was write a poem—an ode
to roadkill

and a decade passed before I knew
I didn't give

permission, the only thing I could control
was my reaction: wide-eyed, limp,
maybe a gasp, maybe a sigh

When the possum plays dead, it enters
a shock stage

It plays such a convincing part
that people have discovered possums this way
and buried them alive

Comatose, its glands produce rotting scents
Green mucus shrouds its body
to repel predators

The laws of predation know
a carcass can't be harmed

the same way a living thing can
Even a predator is afraid of a dead
body in the dark

And then the possum lies still
on an empty road, under stars or pine trees
she'll never see,

until eventually a car comes speeding down the highway
and kills her, this time for real.

from *The Kenyon Review*

Provincetown

◇ ◇ ◇

Fixed at sunset, a wooden blue shack
as if with it a million scenes of shipwrecks,

not black rock or islands of fog rising individual
in a barrenness of salt. It is not that

it was not beautiful, but that I tried to conjure
its momentous light, eternal

that is inside the ordinary, and couldn't. If I look
backwards, the mysteries forming themselves

in darkness, I remember
the heaviness of heat.

A soporific wave lifting from concrete.
There was more a strangeness

in the dark square of water lifting
from a mallard having submerged,

like the sun into water, than there was
to that wooden place. But to think of it

in exile, in its solitude of water,
to see it turn significant

against what could destroy it,
it was then I saw myself becoming it.

from *The Common*

This Is a Love Poem
to Trees

◇　◇　◇

To the sour cherry tree behind our apartment, that summer I made pie and jam.

To the water oak on the coast when you were home waiting, and I said, *Just one more day.*

To the silver maple that waved bare branches twisting gray, when I cried in my childhood bedroom. You and the tree, holding me.

To the linden the summer I was pregnant, and wouldn't that have been a great name for a boy?

Remember that time a raccoon climbed the white pine and built a nest in our dormer, how we wished we could befriend her? The trap in the morning, the drive to the lake, her furry waddle into the woods.

To the woods.

To the tulip tree that wept in early summer, in the new town. The long afternoons I spent alone, drinking tea.

To branches of the old apple tree, alight in your parents' fireplace.

To the weeping willow in Minnesota spring, when I would go for walks and come home, and find you there.

To the mangled green ash outside the window where I sat with our hungry infant. You changed her diapers, and we forgot to touch each other.

To the southern magnolia scenting our neighborhood in Illinois, its fallen leaves brittle as eggshell.

To the bare hickories on our anniversary, ice cream in January, cool sheets and us, alone.

To the hackberry, Siberian elm, river birch, redbud, cottonwood, and aspen. I've loved them all.

To every year the trees grew without us noticing.

from *New Ohio Review*

The Hastily Assembled Angel on Care and Vitality

◇ ◇ ◇

The hastily assembled angel watches

From the air he watches   from that point in the air

Where years from now the apex of the pyra-

mid he is watching being   built will be

Invisibly   he watches as slaves roll

Huge stones from the quarry to the pyramid the

Slave who invented   the method for moving

The stones is dead   the stones   that were too big

For human beings to move   the angel saw

The slave was killed for   attempting to correct

The implementation of his method   which

The Egyptian engineers had not at first

Completely understood   though even as

His dark blood made the dirt beside them dark

They saw the first board buckle   beneath the weight

Of the first stone   fortunately the slave had

Explained his method often to his fellow

Slaves   and they could when they were ordered to

Silently make it work the angel sees the

Slaves serve their masters most   efficiently

When they aren't talking to each other   but

They serve their masters most   quickly just after

They have devised a plan to kill their masters

from *The Yale Review*

There Is Only You

◇   ◇   ◇

That newborn baby smell lingers on my hands palo santo and tap water, molcajete and sábila—and I am now a father. Soy padre. Y ahora el desvelo aparece en los empujones de mi hija. Su voz un parpado de luz. Ave María—esa Luz María, esa mi Lucha, esa mi Lucha, esa es mi lucha.

And I give the baby to my mother and Luz María lets out a bostezo and I see her, I hear
her, I see her, my mother laughs a hard laugh, and mi Lucha wiggles out a smile.

When I walk my parents out of the NICU, my father takes out his flip phone, yes a goddamn flip phone, dials our house in Mejico. ¿Quiúbole padre?, oiga, ahora sí, tenemos raíces acá—nació la herencia, nació la nación y es niña.

My grandfather, que en paz descanse tells me, viejo, guarda ese sentimiento—y que la virgen y los cuatro vientos la protege siempre.

I feel his hand on the back of my neck. I close my eyes for a moment, and I am now entre la luna y mis cerros, the smell of wet earth fills my lungs. For the first time in my life, my heart skips a beat. Mi jefe le dice a mi abuelo, we are bound to this land. This is now his home.

When I walk them to the car, all the words leave me. They speak of when I was a baby and I just listen. All I do now is listen to the coo in my ama's voice, to the caw in my father's jaw, to the hum of mi Lucha's lungs and the rain.

I am filled with listening.

from *Green Mountains Review*

Since Time Immemorial

◇ ◇ ◇

I've heard these words
Spoken repeatedly
As a child
The story of my
Indigenous history shared
With audience after audience
Burnt into my memory
We've been here since time immemorial

It means—time, so long ago
That people have no memory
Or knowledge of it

Filling out my law school application
How long has your family lived in Saskatchewan?
I pause for a moment
Then write
Since time immemorial
What would have been other options?

Since Saskatchewan became a province
Before Saskatchewan was, we were

I was stumped but,

I got in anyway and nobody questioned my answer.

from *Alaska Quarterly Review*

a brief meditation on breath

◊ ◊ ◊

i have diver's lungs from holding my
breath for so long. i promise you
i am not trying to break a record
sometimes i just forget to
exhale. my shoulders held tightly
near my neck, i am a ball of tense
living, a tumbleweed with steel-toed
boots. i can't remember the last time
i felt light as dandelion. i can't remember
the last time i took the sweetness in
& my diaphragm expanded into song.
they tell me breathing is everything,
meaning if i breathe right i can live to be
ancient. i'll grow a soft furry tail or be
telekinetic something powerful enough
to heal the world. i swear i thought
the last time i'd think of death with breath
was that balmy day in july when the cops
became a raging fire & sucked the breath
out of Garner; but yesterday i walked
38 blocks to my father's house with a mask
over my nose & mouth, the sweat dripping
off my chin only to get caught in fabric & pool up
like rain. & i inhaled small spurts of me, little
particles of my dna. i took into body my own self
& thought i'd die from so much exposure
to my own bereavement—they're saying
this virus takes your breath away, not
like a mother's love or like a good kiss

from your lover's soft mouth but like the police
it can kill you fast or slow; dealer's choice.
a pallbearer carrying your body without a casket.
they say it's so contagious it could be quite
breathtaking. so persistent it might as well
be breathing   down your neck—

from Poem-a-Day

Irony

◇ ◇ ◇

It would be now when you feel
want is no longer your enemy,
that your body & soul would kneel.
O it would be now, when you feel
you've culled joy, seized a new zeal
that Death grabs you, fingers icy.
It would be now, when you *feel*!
"Want" is no longer your enemy.

from *The American Poetry Review*

STANLEY MOSS

A Smiling Understanding

◇   ◇   ◇

There is an understanding,
a smiling understanding,
between orchards and orchestras.
Jazz and Bach are fertilizers,
something extra. Trees are much older than music
and poetry. They have bodies and souls,
godlike identities. Trees are choirs,
basso profundos, coloraturas, mezzo sopranos.
I live with music and trees, orchards of music,
woodwinds and sextets. I sing
the "I don't lie to myself" blues.
I learn from my suffering to understand
the suffering of others. I climb musical scales.
Trees have an embouchure. I'm a sapling.
Breath and wind blow through me.
This winter is a coda of falling leaves,
sequoias and maples Louis Armstrong.
I have a band of tree brothers and sisters,
we are not melancholy babies.
I age like a rock, not a rocking chair.
A rock does not wear spectacles, hearing aids,
or use a walking stick. It is dangerous
for anyone to call me "young fellow."

from *The Nation*

When White Hawks Come

◇ ◇ ◇

I dreamt   the spirit of the codfish:

in rafters of the mind;

fly out into the winter's

blue night;

mirth off alder   tendrils sashay;

while I set up

my winter tent;

four panels long—beams suspend

I sit & pull blubber strips   aged in a poke bag;

I'm shadowing the sun   as a new moon icicle

time melts when white   hawks come.

from Poem-a-Day

December

◇　◇　◇

It was never supposed to snow
here, and yet
it was snowing, big flakes tearing down
   over the Edwards Plateau like the sky
            had crumbled. My friend and I drank

         cold wine while our children played
inside with masks
on a big white bed. Another afternoon,
   my daughters sang a song about lords
            and camp that I didn't

         understand, but they didn't like me
to ask what it meant, and
instead of answering rolled down the hill
   in their pajamas. Their
            first secret. Then:

         first bright-red manicure, first
chipped nail, first note taped to the door
saying don't come in. I went
   to the museum instead
            and stared a long time

         at the draft on which Anne Sexton
had scrawled "At last I found you, you funny
old story-poem!" and felt a happy
   envy, happy for her
            but not for me.

Then: first time on ice skates,
chick-chicking around the rink, a string
of beads draped over one daughter's head
    and my gold necklace still tangled
            by the sink. Snow

        rolled over the prairie and held
the fence shadows when we threw
golden hay to the ponies who lived outside
    all winter. The black-and-white barn cat
            was still alive

        and ate nervously in the garage,
where snow chains glittered on the floor. One night
I told a restaurant it was my husband's birthday
    and they gave us a sundae. It was
            his birthday, and at this point

        we were far from the Edwards Plateau.
I can't remember when we left for that trip but I know
on the last day of December we had to go home
and in the airport, waiting for the plane, I arranged
    our winter coats so that mine
            was holding everyone else's.

from *The New Yorker*

Elegy with Table Saw & Cobwebs

◇　◇　◇

Rummaging the wood-rack
I pull a cracked

old shingle off the stack:
a scrap

on which at
some point, with his flat

knife-whittled pencil,
my old friend Ollie scratched

5/32 + 1/2—
a kind of riddle now, a workman's

artifact,
unnoticed since that

year the cancer cells attacked—
since whatever it

once meant,
whatever part it

played in some project,
went with him

into the flames
& ash.

Friends,
we die like that:

the whole starry sky goes black
while these little

nothings last,
while these spiders in the rafters

go on clutching
their white sacks:

whispering & yet & yet
& yet & yet

until I dust the fading rune
& put it back.

from *New England Review*

For Black Children
at the End of the World—
and the Beginning

◇　◇　◇

You are in the black car burning beneath the highway
And rising above it—not as smoke

But what causes it to rise. Hey, Black Child,
You are the fire at the end of your elders'

Weeping, fire against the blur of horse, hoof,
Stick, stone, several plagues including time.

Chrysalis hanging on the bough of this night
And the burning world: *Burn, Baby, burn.*

Anvil and iron be thy name, yea though ye may
Walk among the harnessed heat and huntsmen

Who bear their masters' hunger for paradise
In your rabbit-death, in the beheading of your ghost.

You are the healing snake in the heather
Bursting forth from your humps of sleep.

In the morning, your tongue moves along the earth
Naming hawk sky; rabbit run; your tongue,

Poison to the filthy democracy, to the gold-
Domed capitols where the Guard in their grub-

Worm-colored uniforms cling to the blades of grass—
Worm on the leaf, worm in the dust, worm,

Worm made of rust: sing it with me,
Dragon of Insurmountable Beauty.

Black Child, laugh at the men with their hoofs
and borrowed muscle, their long and short guns,

The worm of their faces, their casket ass-
Embling of the afternoon, left over leaves

From last year's autumn scrapping across their boots;
Laugh, laugh at their assassins on the roofs
(For the time of the assassin is also the time of hysterical laughter).

Black Child, you are the walking-on-of-water
Without the need of an approving master.

You are in a beautiful language.

You are what lies beyond this kingdom
And the next and the next and fire. Fire, Black Child.

from Poem-a-Day

For Air

◇　◇　◇

There is a place in me for air　　as part
of me　　of a piece　　with how I live.
And I am in it making sense like a cart
we are each other's horse before.　　given.

loaded with flowers.　　Both
our breaths　　a fragrance　　of sound wave and beat.
word of the heart.　　The music goes
on to explain it　　is moved by the feet

taking the place apart　　into other places to see.
where is　the surface the air impresses upon
what forms bounce into shape and form
patterns of doing. the way they do that they be.

themselves　　ourselves　　scattered across the drumhead
shod with a vibration of the unsaid.

geometries of air　　shod with a vibration
of the unsaid　　dance out their ordered sentences
to freedom　　the felt articulated into action
a balletic leap　　that seeing　　trails resemblances

of not knowing to knowing　　of silence
to song　　of being bound to flight.
A place in the air achieved　　space—
not even aware the speaking might

be music.   Or that the place of air in us
might be singing   the fragrance of the flowers
already worded   in stone the airy cupolas
of temples lifted off into the idea of showers

of bubbled light   and the poem as the champagne
of what the body has bottled in its strain.

from *Poetry*

Blood

◇ ◇ ◇

Thirty white people wearing white and posing
by the sea. Actually, two of them
wear blue, one of the brothers' wives
who's always trying to distance herself
from the family, and one of her daughters.
It will ruin the picture but better to pretend
nobody notices. First the group shot
then the turns for individual families
who can choose to sit together in the sand
or jump over the surf in unison, grinning.

Every other year, this reunion. All my life.
The same photographer shoots it
wearing her son's old cargo shorts.
Something bad had happened to her, maybe
I wasn't told. And it made her
not as you'd expect a tragedy would
make someone but cheerful, capable.
Last year, she got married.

Last year, whatever I was doing
on the beach, I was thinking
about a man. When he was
with me, he was cheating on the woman
he was cheating on his girlfriend with.
But the woman was going to
have a baby and he told me he
was leaving me and the girlfriend both
to be with her, it.

The little cousins walked
the sand at night with flashlights
to detect the crabs they shoveled
into plastic pails they'd carry out as far
as they could walk, then dump there.

The one aunt who was single
would describe herself as married
to Christ. "And we have fights
like any couple." When a cousin
turned thirteen, she took them
on a beach walk to explain chastity.
She was a Shakespeare scholar
who discovered in the tragedies
some details at the ends which indicated
wretched characters were born again.

Some things everyone agreed on, like
you had to justify a garment praised
by saying how cheap it was.
In other cases, no one felt the same.
When giving punishments, for instance,
whether somebody who'd been bad
should sit alone reflecting in a room
or apologize to the group and whether
or not to soothe somebody
who had torn their clothes off, sobbing.

The cottages we rented on the shore
weren't part of any family's real life.
They were designed to feel
they had no history. It was comfortable.
Even the plates and cups we used
were all disposable, though the silverware
was metal. Bright flags of beach towels
draped over the porch railing.
Standing by them, you could barely see
the water for the roofs of other rentals.

When they were sunburned,
the aunts drove to a market
selling handmade soap and straw hats, delicate
cheap jewelry. An uncle said
the site had been a slave market.
His wife said please don't tell the kids that.

They lived, like most of us, in the middle
of the country, two days drive away.
He brought from home a giant pool float
so we could ride the ocean. Over and over, waves
shot it forward and you fell off screaming
or kept clinging to it somehow, screaming.
We called it Party Barge and marveled daily
at its not puncturing.

Each year, the pictures taken on the beach
would turn out brighter, more
garish than the twilit shore
remembered. Inland, one year
hung beside the other, framed, detached,
as if history were comprised of do-overs.
The dress code always white, white
and tan, and some of the same
shirts and dresses would appear again.

Before the reunion, I was
with the man at my parents' apartment
on a bed that used to be my sister's.
Next to it, the built-in shelves
still crowded with dolls she liked
to line up on the floor and count.

When I got home, he said
the woman lost the baby
so he felt free to love me.

from *The Yale Review*

brown and black people
on shark tank

◇   ◇   ◇

We are seeking one million dollars for 12% of our stories. This product will revolutionize the industry. We are revolutionaries. We are evolutionaries. I used to work in the restaurant business. I graduated from Harvard, Yale, and Princeton with a BA, MBA, PhD from all three. I'm a sophomore in college. I'm in high school. I'm 10 years old. I haven't been born yet. My family told me I wasn't going to make it. My family was very supportive. Yes, there is a need for this product in our communities. Yes, people have curly hair in our communities. Yes, people die in our communities. Yes, this is an original recipe. Yes, my mother gave it to me. She died single-handedly saving a burning bus full of orphans on I-95. No, there's no product like this on the market yet. No, this isn't a niche product. I mean there is a large niche for this product. Yes, there is a need for this kind of product. No, this product isn't exclusively for my community. I am not being exclusive. I've never been exclusive. I have never been excluded. Yes, I'm sure anyone can use this product. Yes, anyone with hair or heart or nails or feet can use this product. Yes, the margins are high enough. Yes, we're cash flow positive. Yes, my people have money. Yes, my parents had money. I'm a hard worker. If you tell me to jump, I'll fly. I'll quit my job. I'll quit my wife. I'll quit my life. My family came here with no money. My family has no money. My money has no money. I'm worth it, I promise. You won't regret it. I believe in this product. I believe in this brand so much. I want money, not a loan and here's a story about the time my dad took a loan out and we couldn't eat for the next ten years. Please take a chance on us. I believe in me. I believe in America. We're sorry to hear that you're out. Thank you thank you thank you.

from *Pigeon Pages*

NICOLE SEALEY

Pages 5–8 (An excerpt from The Ferguson Report: An Erasure)

◇ ◇ ◇

City **officials** have frequently asserted that the harsh and disparate results of Ferguson's law enforcement system do not indicate problems with police or court practices, but instead reflect a pervasive lack of "personal responsibility" among "certain segments" of the community. Our investigation has **found** that the practices about which area residents have complained are in fact unconstitutional and unduly harsh. But the City's personal-responsibility refrain is telling.

It reflects many of the same racial stereotypes found in the emails between police and court supervisors. This evidence of bias and stereotyping, together with evidence that Ferguson has long recognized but failed to correct the consistent racial disparities caused by its police and c **our** t practices, demonstrates that the discriminatory effects of Ferguson's **conduct** are driven at least in part by discriminatory intent in violation of the Fourteenth Amendment.

Community Distrust

Since the August 2014 shooting death of Michael Brown, the lack of trust between the Ferguson Police Department and a significant portion of Ferguson's residents, especially African Americans, has become undeniable. The **cause** s of this distrust and division, however, have been the subject of debate. Police and other City **official** s, as well as some Ferguson residents, have insisted to us that the public outcry is attributable to "outside agitators" who do not reflect the opinions of "real Ferguson residents." That view is at odds with the facts we have gathered during our investigation. Our investigation has shown that distrust of the Ferguson Police Department is longstanding and largely attributable to Ferguson's approach to law enforcement. This approach results in patterns of unnecessarily aggressive and at times unlawful policing; reinforces the **harm** of discriminatory stereotypes; discourages a culture of accountability; and neglects community engagement. In recent years, FPD has moved away from the modest community policing efforts it previously had implemented, reducing opportunities for positive police-community interactions, and losing the little familiarity it had with some African-American neighborhoods. The confluence of policing to raise revenue and racial bias thus has resulted in practices that not only violate the Constitution and cause direct harm to the individuals whose rights are violated, but also undermine community trust, especially among many African Americans. As a consequence of these practices, law enforcement is seen as illegitimate, and the partnerships necessary for public safety are, in some areas, entirely absent.

Restoring trust in law enforcement will require recognition of the harms caused by Ferguson's law enforcement practices, and diligent, committed collaboration with the entire Ferguson community. At the conclusion of this report, we have broadly identified the changes that are necessary for meaningful and sustainable reform. These measures build upon a number of other recommended changes we communicated verbally to the Mayor, Police Chief, and City Manager in September so that Ferguson could begin immediately to address problems as we identified them. As a result of those recommendations, the City and police department have already begun to make some changes to municipal court and police practices. We commend City **officials** for beginning to take steps to address some of the concerns we have already raised. Nonetheless, these changes are only a small part of the reform necessary. Addressing the deeply embedded constitutional deficiencies we **found** demands an entire reorientation of law enforcement in Ferg**us**on. The City must replace revenue-driven policing with a system grounded in the principles of community policing and police legitimacy, in which people are equally protected and treated with compassion, regardless of race.

II. BACKGROUND

The City of Ferguson is one of 89 municipalities in St. Louis County, Missouri. According to United St**at**es Census Data from 2010, Ferguson is

home to roughly 21,000 residents. While Ferguson's total populat**i**o**n** has stayed relatively constant in recent decades, Ferguson's racial demographics have changed dramatically during that time. In 1990, 74% of Ferguson's population was white, while 25% was black. By 2000, African Americans became the new majority, making up 52% of the City's population. According to the 2010 Census, the black population in Ferguson has grown to 67%, whereas the white population has decreased to 29%. According to the 2009-2013 American Community Survey, 25% of the City's population lives below the federal poverty level.

Residents of Ferguson elect a Mayor and six individuals to serve on a City Council. **The** City Council appoints a City Manager to an indefinite term, subject to removal by a Council vote. *See* Ferguson City Charter § 4.1. The City Manager serves as chief executive and administrative officer of the City of Ferguson, and is responsible for all affairs of the City. The City Manager directs and supervises all City departments, including the Ferguson Police Department.

The current Chief of Police, Thomas Jackson, has commanded the police department since he was appointed by the City Manager in 2010. The department has a total of 54 sworn officers divided among several divisions. The patrol division is the largest division; 28 patrol officers are supervised by four sergeants, two lieutenants, and a captain. Each of the four patrol squads has a canine officer. While all patrol officers engage in traffic enforcement, FPD also has a dedicated traffic officer responsible for collecting traffic stop data required by the state of Missouri. FPD has two School Resource Officers ("SROs"), one who is assigned to the McCluer South-Berkeley High School and one who is assigned to the Ferguson Middle School. FPD has a single officer assigned to be the "Community Resource Officer," who attends community meetings, serves as FPD's public relations liaison, and is charged with collecting crime data. FPD operates its own jail, which has ten individual cells and a large holding cell. The jail is staffed by three non-sworn correctional officers. Of the 54 sworn officers currently serving in FPD, four are African American.

FPD officers are authorized to initiate charges—by issuing citations or summonses, or by making arrests—under both the municipal code and state law. Ferguson's municipal code addresses nearly every aspect of civic life for those who live in Ferguson, and regulates the conduct of all who work, travel through, or otherwise visit the City. In addition to mirroring some non-felony state law

violations, such as assault, stealing, and traffic violations, the code establishes housing violations, such as **High Grass** and Weeds; requirements for permits to rent an apartment or use the City's trash service; animal control ordinances, such as Barking Dog and Dog Running at Large; and a number of other violations, such as Manner of Walking in Roadway. See, e.g., Ferguson Mun. Code §§ 29-16 et seq.; 37-1 et seq.; 46-27; 6-5, 6-11; 44-344.

FPD files most charges as municipal offenses, not state violations, even when an analogous state offense exists. Between July 1, 2010, and June 30, 2014, the City of Ferguson issued approximately 90,000 citations and summonses for municipal violations. Notably, the City issued nearly 50% more citations in the last year of that time period than it did in the first. This increase in enforcement has not been driven by a rise in serious crime. While the ticketing rate has increased dramatically, the number of charges for many of the most serious offenses covered by the municipal code—e.g., Assault, Driving While Intoxicated, and Stealing—has remained relatively constant.

Because the overwhelming majority of FPD's enforcement actions are brought under the municipal code, most charges are processed and resolved by the Ferguson Municipal Court, which has primary jurisdiction over all code violations. Ferguson Mun. Code § 13-2. Ferguson's municipal court operates as part of the police department. The court is supervised by the Ferguson Chief of Police, is considered part of the police department for City organizational purposes, and is physically located within the police station. Court staff report directly to the Chief of Police. Thus, if the City Manager or other City officials issue a court-related directive, it is typically sent to the Police Chief's attention. In recent weeks, City officials informed us that they are considering plans to bring the court under the supervision of the City Finance Director.

A Municipal Judge presides over court sessions. The Municipal Judge is not hired or supervised by the Chief of Police, but is instead nominated by the City Manager and elected by the City Council. The Judge serves a two-year term, subject to reappointment. The current Municipal Judge, Ronald Brockmeyer, has presided in Ferguson for approximately ten years. The City's Prosecuting Attorney and her assistants officially prosecute all actions before the court, although in practice most cases are resolved without trial or a prosecutor's involvement. The current Prosecuting Attorney was appointed in April 2011. At the time of her appointment, the Prosecuting Attorney was already serving as City Attorney, and she continues to serve in that separate capacity, which entails providing general counsel and representation to the City. The Municipal Judge, Court Clerk, Prosecuting Attorney, and all assistant court clerks are white.

While the Municipal Judge presides over court sessions, the Court Clerk, who is employed under the Police Chief's supervision, plays the most significant role in managing the court and exercises broad discretion in conducting the court's daily operations. Ferguson's municipal code confers broad authority on the Court Clerk, including the authority to collect all fines and fees,

accept guilty pleas, sign and issue subpoenas, and approve bond determinations. Ferguson Mun. Code § 13-7. Indeed, the Court Clerk and assistant clerks routinely perform duties that are, for all practical purposes, judicial. For example, documents indicate that court clerks have disposed of charges without the Municipal Judge's involvement.

The court officially operates subject to the oversight of the presiding judge of the St. Louis County Circuit Court (21st Judicial Circuit) under the rules promulgated by that Circuit Court and the Missouri Supreme Court. Notwithstanding these rules, the City of Ferguson and the court itself retain considerable power to establish and amend court practices and procedures. The Ferguson municipal code sets forth a limited number of protocols that the court must follow, but the code leaves most aspects of court operations to the discretion of the court itself. See Ferguson Mun. Code Ch. 13, Art. III. The code also explicitly authorizes the Municipal Judge to "make and adopt such rules of practice and procedure as are necessary to hear and decide matters pending before the municipal court." Ferguson Mun. Code § 13-29.

The Ferguson Municipal Court has the authority to issue and enforce judgments, issue warrants for search and arrest, hold parties in contempt, and order imprisonment as a penalty for contempt. The court may conduct trials, although it does so rarely, and most charges are resolved without one. Upon resolution of a charge, the court has the authority to impose fines, fees, and imprisonment when violations are found. Specifically, the court can impose imprisonment in the Ferguson City Jail for up to three months, a fine of up to $1,000, or a combination thereof. It is rare for the court to sentence anyone to jail as a penalty for a violation of the municipal code; indeed, the Municipal Judge reports that he has done so only once.

Rather, the court almost always imposes a monetary penalty payable to the City of Ferguson, plus court fees. Nonetheless, as discussed in detail below, the court issues arrest warrants when a person misses a court appearance or fails to timely pay a fine. As a result, violations that would normally not result in a penalty of imprisonment can, and frequently do, lead to municipal warrants, arrests, and jail time.

As the number of charges initiated by FPD has increased in recent years, the size of the court's docket has also increased. According to data the City reported to the Missouri State Courts Administrator, at the end of fiscal year 2009, the municipal court had roughly 24,000 traffic cases and 28,000 non-traffic cases pending. As of October 31, 2014, both of those figures had roughly doubled to 53,000 and 50,000 cases, respectively. In fiscal year 2009, 16,178 new cases were filed, and 8,727 were resolved. In 2014, by contrast, 24,256 new offenses were filed, and 10,975 offenses were resolved.

The court holds three or four sessions per month, and each session lasts no more than three hours. It is not uncommon for as many as 500 people to appear before the court in a single session, exceeding the court's physical capacity and leading individuals to line up outside of court waiting to be heard. Many people have multiple offenses pending; accordingly, the court typically considers 1,200–1,500 offenses in a single session, and has in the past considered over 2,000 offenses during one sitting. Previously there was a cap on the number of offenses that could be assigned to a particular docket date. Given that cap, and the significant increase in municipal citations in recent years, a problem developed in December 2011 in which more citations were issued than court sessions could timely accommodate. At one point court dates were initially scheduled as far as six months after the date of the citation. To address this problem, court staff first raised the cap to allow 1,000 offenses to be assigned to a single court date and later eliminated the cap altogether. To handle the increasing caseload, the City Manager also requested and secured City Council approval to fund additional court positions, noting in January 2013 that "each month we are setting new all-time records in fines and forfeitures," that this was overburdening court staff, and that the funding for the additional positions "will be more than covered by the increase in revenues."

III. FERGUSON LAW ENFORCEMENT EFFORTS ARE FOCUSED ON GENERATING REVENUE

City officials have consistently set maximizing revenue as the priority for Ferguson's law enforcement activity. Ferguson generates a significant and increasing amount of revenue from the enforcement of code provisions. The City has budgeted for, and achieved, significant increases in revenue from municipal code enforcement over the last several years, and these increases are projected to continue. Of the $11.07 million in general fund revenue the City collected in fiscal year 2010, $1.38 million came from fines and fees collected by the court; similarly, in fiscal year 2011, the City's general fund revenue of $11.44 million included $1.41 million from fines and fees. In its budget for fiscal year 2012, however, the City predicted that revenue from municipal fines and fees would increase over 30% from the previous year's amount to

$1.92 million; the court exceeded that target, collecting $2.11 million. In its budget for fiscal year 2013, the City budgeted for fines and fees to yield $2.11 million; the court exceeded that target as well, collecting $2.46 million. For 2014, the City budgeted for the municipal court to generate $2.63 million in revenue. The City has not yet made public the actual revenue collected that year, although budget documents forecasted lower revenue than was budgeted. Nonetheless, for fiscal year 2015, the City's budget anticipates fine and fee revenues to account for $3.09 million of a projected $13.26 million in general fund revenues.

City, police, and court officials for years have worked in concert to maximize revenue at every stage of the enforcement process, beginning with how fines and fine enforcement processes are established. In a February 2011 report requested by the City Council at a Financial Planning Session and drafted by Ferguson's Finance Director with contributions from Chief Jackson, the Finance Director reported on "efforts to increase efficiencies and maximize collection" by the municipal court. The report included an extensive comparison of Ferguson's fines to those of surrounding municipalities and noted with approval that Ferguson's fines are "at or near the top of the list." The chart noted, for example, that while other municipalities' parking fines generally range from $5 to $100, Ferguson's is $102. The chart noted also that the charge for "Weeds/Tall Grass" was as little as $5 in one city but, in Ferguson, it ranged form $77 to $102. The report stated that the acting prosecutor had reviewed the City's "high volume offenses" and "started recommending higher fines on these cases, and recommending probation only infrequently." While the report stated that this

from *The Paris Review*

women's voting rights
at one hundred
(but who's counting?)

◇　◇　◇

eenie meenie minie moe
catch a voter by her toe
if she hollers then you know
got yourself a real jane crow

★★★

one vote is an opinion
with a quiet legal force ::
a barely audible beep
in the local traffic, & just
a plashless drop of mercury
in the national thermometer.
but a collectivity of votes
/*a flock of votes, a pride of votes,*
a murder of votes/can really
make some noise.

★★★

one vote begets another
if you make a habit of it.
my mother started taking me
to the polls with her when i

was seven :: small, thrilled
to step in the booth, pull
the drab curtain hush-shut
behind us, & flip the levers
beside each name she pointed
to, the Xs clicking into view.
there, she called the shots.

★★★

rich gal, poor gal
hired girl, thief
teacher, journalist
vote your grief

★★★

one vote's as good as another
:: still, in 1913, illinois's gentle
suffragists, hearing southern
women would resent spotting
mrs. ida b. wells-barnett amidst
whites marchers, gently kicked
their sister to the curb. but when
the march kicked off, ida got
right into formation, as planned.
the *tribune*'s photo showed
her present & accounted for.

★★★

one vote can be hard to keep
an eye on :: but several /a
colony of votes/ can't scuttle
away unnoticed so easily. my
mother, veteran registrar for
our majority black election
district, once found—after
much searching—two bags

of ballots /*a litter of votes*/
stuffed in a janitorial closet.

★★★

one-mississippi
two-mississippis

★★★

one vote was all fannie lou
hamer wanted. in 1962, when
her constitutional right was
over forty years old, she tried
to register. all she got for her
trouble was literacy tested, poll
taxed, fired, evicted, & shot
at. a year of grassroots activism
nearly planted her mississippi
freedom democratic party
in the national convention.

★★★

one vote per eligible voter
was all stacey abrams needed.
she nearly won the georgia
governor's race in 2018 :: lost by
50,000 /*an unkindness of votes*/
to the man whose job was ~~purg~~
maintaining the voter rolls.
days later, she rolled out plans
for getting voters a fair fight.
it's been two years—& counting.

from *American Poets*

What Is There to Do in Akron, Ohio?

◊   ◊   ◊

complain about the weather. wait five minutes
watch the boys you grew up with outgrow you
bury your cousin. go sledding on the tallest hill you can find
keep a family warm until their son thaws out of prison
ice skate between the skyscrapers downtown
inherit an emergency exit sign from your father
spray paint your best friend's brother on a t-shirt
daydream your way through a semester-long funeral
watch jeans and sleeves and family portraits unravel
play soccer with the black boys who almost evaporated
with the icicles. kick it outside with the skeletons
from your childhood. go to columbus and pretend
to be a grownup. spend a weekend at kalahari resort
and call it a vacation. go back home. leave. shoot dice
with the dead boys playing dress up. stay long enough
to become a tourist attraction in a city nobody stops in
mount bikes and ride until the sun dribbles
out of the sky's mouth. wade through the oatmeal july makes
of morning air. swim in a public pool where everyone
is drowning and no one knows how to survive
what happened last month. *stop runnin in and out* unless
you got somethin' on the gas bill. seal yourself with cold air
while the trees melt. bet the boy down the street that you'll have
the best *first day* fit. come out amid orange leaves lookin' fresher
than all the food in a 5-mile radius of granny's house
eat jojos from rizzi's on sunday after pastor guilt trips you
on your way past the pulpit. dream about a city

where headstones don't show up to dinner unannounced
where fried chicken isn't on speed dial and diabetes
isn't the family heirloom. where grief isn't so molasses
root for lebron in whatever he's wearing. become
an athlete as a way out of corner sales. never escape.
start a pickup game that never ends. rake leaves
with a rusted afro pick your older brother left you in his will
let the leaf bags melt into the chimney on the side of the house
play basketball with the ghosts who don't know what year it is
volunteer at your local funeral home. open a cemetery
across the street from the playground. mow green
cut ties with your grass-seller. survive the summer.

from *New Ohio Review*

PATRICIA SMITH

The Stuff of Astounding:
A Golden Shovel
for Juneteenth

◊ ◊ ◊

Unless you spring from a history that is smug and reckless, unless
you've vowed yourself blind to a ceaseless light, you see us. We
are a shea-shined toddler writhing through Sunday sermon, we are
the grizzled elder gingerly unfolding his last body. And we are intent
and insistent upon the human in ourselves. We are the doctor on
another day at the edge of reason, coaxing a wrong hope, ripping
open a gasping body to find air. We are five men dripping from the
burly branches of young trees, which is to say that we dare a world
that is both predictable and impossible. What else can we learn from
suicides of the cuffed, the soft targets black backs be? Stuck in its
rhythmic unreel, time keeps including us, even as our aged root
is doggedly plucked and trampled, cursed by ham-fisted spitters in
the throes of a particular fever. See how we push on as enigma, the
free out loud, the audaciously unleashed, how slyly we scan the sky—
all that wet voltage and scatters of furious star—to realize that we
are the recipients of an ancient grace. No, we didn't *begin* to live

when, on the 19th June day of that awkward, ordinary spring—with no joy, in a monotone still flecked with deceit—*Seems you and these others are free*. That moment did not begin our breath. Our truths— the ones we'd been birthed with—had already met reckoning in the fields as we muttered tangled nouns of home. We reveled in black from there to now, our rampant hue and nap, the unbridled breath that resides in the rafters, from then to here, everything we are is the stuff of astounding. We are a mother who hums snippets of gospel into the silk curls of her newborn, we are the harried sister on the elevator to the weekly paycheck mama dreamed for her. We are black in every way there is—perm and kink, upstart and elder, wide voice, fervent whisper. We heft our clumsy homemade placards, we will curl small in the gloom weeping to old blues ballads. We swear not to be anybody else's idea of free, lining up precisely, waiting to be freed again and again. We are breach and bellow, resisting a silent consent as we claim our much of America, its burden and snarl, the stink and hallelujah of it, its sicknesses and safe words, all its black and otherwise. Only those feigning blindness fail to see the body of work we are, and the work of body we have done. Everything is what it is because of us. It is misunderstanding to believe that free fell upon us like a blessing, that it was granted by a signature and an abruptly opened door. Listen to the thousand ways to say *black* out loud. Hear a whole people celebrate their free and fragile lives, then find your own place inside that song. Make the singing matter.

from *The New York Times*

Ode to the Boy Who Jumped Me

◊   ◊   ◊

You and your friend stood
on the corner of the liquor store
as I left Champa Garden,

takeout in hand, on the phone
with Ashley who said,
That was your tough voice.

I never heard your tough voice before.
I gave you boys a quick nod,
walked E 21st past dark houses.

Before I could reach the lights
on Park, you criss-crossed
your hands around me,

like a friend and I'd hoped
that you were Seng,
the boy I'd kissed on First Friday

in October. He paid for my lunch
at that restaurant, split the leftovers.
But that was a long time ago

and we hadn't spoken since,
so I dropped to my knees
to loosen myself from your grip,

my back to the ground, I kicked
and screamed but nobody
in the neighborhood heard me,

only Ashley on the other line,
in Birmingham, where they say
How are you? to strangers

not what I said in my tough voice
but what I last texted Seng,
no response. You didn't get on top,

you hovered. My elbows banged
the sidewalk. I threw
the takeout at you and saw

your face. Young. More scared
of me than I was of you.
Hands on my ankles, I thought

you'd take me or rape me.
Instead you acted like a man
who slipped out of my bed

and promised to call:
You said nothing.
Not even what you wanted.

from Poem-a-Day

Chinese Restaurant
Syndrome

◇　◇　◇

The notion that the children, awaiting dumplings,
will never know their grandparents.

The chance that the Peking duck, though crispy
and succulent, is not the artist's medium.

The likelihood that your hometown stopped existing
before you knew this would be permanent.

Being recognized each time. The possibility
that the place will be robbed, due to location,

its spurning of credit. The years that have passed
since you saw your uncles. The gratitude

with which you clean your house, placeless
and beautiful. The safety of your neighborhood.

The ritual by which friends who share your heritage
fight for the check. The appreciation of friends

who do not, as you explain the pickled cabbage,
the absence of fish from fish-fragrance. The hands

of two women in a corner booth, shelling peas.
Roast pork like your grandmother's, in vast portions.

The assumption that rice and tea are always free.
Your children growing up, seeking their fortunes.

from *Bennington Review*

Acequia del Llano

◇ ◇ ◇

1

The word *acequia* is derived from the Arabic *as-saqiya* (water conduit)
and refers to an irrigation ditch that transports water from a river to
farms and fields, as well as the association of members connected to it.

> Blossoming peach trees—
> to the west, steel buildings glint
> above the mesa.

In Santa Fe, New Mexico, the Acequia del Llano is one and a half
miles long and begins at Nichols Reservoir dam. At the bottom of
the dam, an outlet structure and flow meter control water that runs
through a four-inch pipe at up to one hundred-fifty gallons per
minute. The water runs along a hillside and eventually drops into
the Santa Fe River. Fifteen families and two organizations belong to
this ditch association, and the acequia irrigates about thirty acres of
gardens and orchards.

> In the ditch, water flowing—
> now an eagle-feather wind.

2

Yarrow, rabbitbrush, claret cup cactus, one-seed juniper, Douglas fir,
and scarlet penstemon are some of the plants in this environment.
Endangered and threatened species include the southwestern willow

flycatcher, the least tern, the violet-crowned hummingbird, the American marten, and the white-tailed ptarmigan.

> Turning my flashlight
> behind me, I see a large
> buck, three feet away.

Each April, all of the members come, or hire workers who come, to do the annual spring cleaning; this involves walking the length of the ditch, using shovels and clippers to clear branches, silt, and other debris.

> Twigs, pine needles, plastic bags
> cleared today before moonrise—

3

The ditch association is organized with a *mayordomo*, ditch manager, who oversees the distribution of water according to each *parciante*'s (holder of water rights) allotment. The acequia runs at a higher elevation than all of the land held by the *parciantes*, so the flow of water is gravity fed.

> Crisscrossing the ditch,
> avoiding cholla,
> I snag my hair on branches.

Each year the irrigation season runs from about April 15 to October 15. On Thursdays and Sundays, at 5:30 a.m., I get up and walk about a quarter of a mile uphill to the ditch and drop a metal gate into it. When the water level rises, water goes through screens then down two pipes and runs below to irrigate grass, lilacs, trees, and an orchard.

> Across the valley, ten lights
> glimmer from hillside houses.

Orion and other constellations of stars stand out at that hour. As it moves toward summer, the constellations shift, and, by July 1, when I walk uphill, I walk in early daylight. By mid-September, I again go uphill in the dark and listen for coyote and deer in between the piñons and junipers.

> One by one, we light
> candles on leaves, let them go
> flickering downstream.

The Ganges River is 1,569 miles long. The Rio Grande is 1,896 miles long; it periodically dries up, but when it runs its full length, it runs from its headwaters in the mountains of southern Colorado into the Gulf of Mexico. Water from the Santa Fe River runs into the Rio Grande. Water from the Acequia del Llano runs into the Santa Fe River. From a length of one hundred paces along the acequia, I draw our allotment of water.

> Here, I pull a translucent
> cactus spine out of your hand.

from *The Kenyon Review*

Copernicus

◇   ◇   ◇

Who doesn't know how
doubt lifts the hem of its nightgown

to reveal another inch of thigh
before the face of faith?

I once didn't. I once thought I was
my own geometry,
my own geocentric planet

spinning like a ballerina, alone
at the center of the universe, at the command of a god
opening my music box
with his dirty mouth. He said

Let there be light—
And I thought I was the light.

I was a man's failed imagination.

Now I know what appears
as the motion of Heaven
is just the motion of Earth.

Not stars.
Not whatever I want.

from *The New Yorker*

The Beginning
of the Beginning

◊ ◊ ◊

Who decides where a river starts? When are there enough
sources, current strong and water wide enough for its name?

In Colorado, the Chama begins in smaller creeks and streams,
flows into New Mexico to form the Rio Grande, splitting Texas

and Mexico (who decided?) and moves deeper south. I think
these thoughts by a creek on a beating hot day,

as water rips by in rapids propelled, formed in mountains far above.
The water icy even in this summer heat. People grin

some false bravery, scared to sit in tubes and dip into the tide
to be carried away. I think of drowning. Of who sees water

as fun. Who gets to play in a heatwave. Who trusts
the flow. Migrants floating in the Rio Grande haunt me, so

I think of families tired of waiting, of mercy that never comes,
of taking back Destiny. The rivers must have claimed more

this year. Know no metering but the rush of their mountain
source's melt. A toddling child follows her father into water's

pull. Think of gang's demands, of where those come from. Trickles
of needs meeting form a flow of migrants. Think of where

it begins. Think of the current of history—long, windy, but traceable and forceful in its early shapes.

from *The American Poetry Review*

The Dead Just Need
to Be Seen. Not Forgiven

◊   ◊   ◊

That old man in the photo our family never talks about,
known best for tracking runaway slaves; tonight

we drag him from the basement up these loose
wood stairs & set out a plate of salted cabbage & rabbit—

so long since I've asked why the empty chair at our table.
With all the warmth a body has to give, we give up on

measuring the darkness between men. Dust & dusk enter
& are wiped from the room. The names we call each other

linger luminous & savage. Still. That tree I used to hang
tires from holds tight its dead centuries. The light

swinging from its branches we call rope-like,
which implies there's no longer rope. Tonight, we'll wash

the burnt-out stars from his hair, all the crumbs from his beard.
The misfired bullet of his voice we let burn as it must.

from *Southern Indiana Review*

Red Wine Spills

◇ ◇ ◇

I am hovering over this rug
with a hair dryer on high in my hand
I have finally, inevitably, spilled
red wine on this impractically white
housewarming hand-me-down from my cousin, who
clearly, and incorrectly, thought this was a good idea

With the help of a little panic,
sparkling water and a washcloth,
I am stunned by how quickly the wine washes out,
how I was sure this mistake would find me
every day with its gaping mouth, reminding me
of my own propensity for failure
and yet, here I am
with this clean slate

The rug is made of fur,
which means it died
to be here

It reminds me of my own survival
and everyone who has taught me
to shake loose the shadow of death

I think of inheritance, how this rug
was passed on to me through blood,
how this animal gave its blood
so that I may receive the gift of its death
and be grateful for it

I think of our inability
to control stories of origin
how history does not wash away
with water and a good scrub

I think of evolution,
what it means to make it through
this world with your skin intact,
how flesh is fragile
but makes a needle and thread
of itself when necessary

I think of all that I have inherited,
all the bodies buried for me to be here
and stay here, how I was born with grief
and gratitude in my bones

And I think of legacy,
how I come from a long line of sorcerers
who make good work of building
joy from absolutely nothing

And what can I do with that
but pour another glass,
thank the stars
for this sorceress blood
and keep pressing forward

from Poem-a-Day

SHELLEY WONG

How to Live
in Southern California

◊   ◊   ◊

Stay in the car and move from one air-conditioned location
        to another chill location, perhaps in a tour of movie theaters.
After a long winter back east, 76 percent of California's population

        is facing abnormal dryness or drought. My family went
                to Palos Verdes to look for gray whales, where the water was rough
and edged with mansions. As of June 19, 2018, 3 percent

        is affected by extreme or exceptional drought. The Pacific Ocean
                is a stage for an altar or a talk show. On the boat, my mother said,
"Don't turn your back on the ocean." Drive down Pacific Coast Highway

        in a long, curving line—past sandal palaces, neon seafood shacks,
                and offshore oil rigs—while listening to Fleetwood Mac, Katy Perry,
and Frank Ocean. Since the 1800s, my family has lived

        along the West Coast, from Seattle to San Francisco to Long Beach,
                where the sun so often set without our watching. Come to Disneyland,
the Hollywood sign, to paradise-by-the-highway. At 3 a.m., there's always

        another milkshake, another strike to roll in the bowling alley
                of an Art Deco hotel. After discussing polygamy in Utah in 1875,
President Ulysses S. Grant said, "I invite the attention of Congress

        to another, though perhaps no less an evil—the importation
                of Chinese women, but few of whom are brought to our shores
to pursue honorable or useful occupations." The spectrum of drought conditions

is color-coded from yellow to dark red. In Los Angeles, people drive
              for the experience of driving, to be at the beach and in the hills
within the same hour. The drought website is maintained

              by the National Drought Mitigation Center. Walk out
              to the end of the pier. The good life is when you don't feel
the weather. With sunglasses, you own a particular glamour.

from *The Kenyon Review*

Overnight

◇   ◇   ◇

In Memory of Paul Violi (1944–2011)

I did not realize that you were fading from sight
I don't believe I could have helped with the transition

You most likely would have made a joke of it
Did you hear about the two donkeys stuck in an airshaft

I don't believe I could have helped with the transition
The doorway leading to the valleys of dust is always open

Did you hear about the two donkeys stuck in an airshaft
You might call this the first of many red herrings

The doorway leading to the valleys of dust is always open
The window overlooking the sea is part of the dream

You might call this the first of many red herrings
The shield you were given as a child seldom worked

The window overlooking the sea is part of the dream
One by one the words leave you, even this one

The shield you were given as a child seldom worked
The sword is made of air before you knew it

One by one the words leave you, even this one
I did not realize that you were fading from sight

The sword is made of air before you knew it
You most likely would have made a joke of it

from *Hambone*

Caution (from "Deracinations: Seven Sonigrams")

◊ ◊ ◊

Frisky, her canine sidekick,
(she'd named him when she was 6),

had taken off again, seeing his chance
when she let him out to urinate,

tunneling under the cedar stakes
of the fence (as was his much-denounced

tendency) to make his social rounds
of the neighborhood. She sighed.

It was 10pm on Saturday night,
her parents were at the Korean church

for choir practice, and, conscientious,
she couldn't let the dog run loose

all night (not since he, contrite,
had once returned with an unsigned

note duct-taped to his collar: *I'll shoot
this fucking dog if I see him in my yard!*)

Honestly, Frisky, though cute,
was a pain in the ass. Untrained,

he had the bad habit of chasing
mail carriers, acquaintances (once

he knocked a pregnant stranger
off her bike). Only Asians, for some reason,

were exempt from these attacks.
He thinks we all look alike,

they tittered. She knew, that night,
where he was: the faux-Tudor estate

across the lake: the Coates' residence.
She was in homeroom with their son, Trey.

The cool kids had handed around
fliers for a kegger at the Coates'

that Saturday, advertising a set
by his band White Minority (Trey

was both lead guitar *and* lead singer).
Frisky, though half her size (and,

moreover, spayed) nonetheless
liked to sniff around the Coates'

German shepherd, Bitch (that
was her name. Ha ha.) She didn't

want to knock at the front door,
asking for her dog, endure the sneers,

awkward, avoiding eye contact,
while they searched the dog out.

She didn't want to crouch
down in front of them to attach

the leash—the scenario nauseated her.
Luckily, another course of action

occurred to her: she could row across
the lake in her family's canoe,

skulk across the yard unnoticed
till she located the truant,

return to her own home, unseen.
Nonetheless, she put on eyeshadow,

lipgloss, a cute (but not *too* cute)
top. Best to be inconspicuous,

she dissembled. (She cherished
a secret crush on Trey, unconfessed

even to herself.) Her trusty canoe cut
through the darkness—her destination

shining like a signal fire. She docked.
What the fucking fuck? A semi-nude

couple in an Adirondack chair
cussed her out, then carried on.

The amber floodlight scattered
citrines across a swathe of dark grass.

The yellow brick road, she thought,
skirting it. *Friiiiiisky!* she hissed.

By the poolhouse the dog, serene
for once, luxuriated—an odalisque.

His tail smacked the concrete
like a slow clap. *You idiot,*

she scolded, snapped on
the leash, retraced her route.

Another curse from the now entirely
unclothed interrupted inamorati,

but otherwise their surreptitious exit
passed undetected. Success!

Home by 10:30, well in advance
of her unsuspecting parents' return. Not

till Monday did she learn the sequence
of events later . . . much later . . . that night:

a dirty-blond teenaged girl with "issues,"
with clear indicators of "ideation"

(a new term-of-art to her)—that is,
according to the Coates. A drunken

semi-conscious round of Russian roulette
(usually, even at the hardest-core

gatherings, understood to be charade.)
But this time, the game was both truth

and dare. "A tragic accident,"
the principal said, when she cut short

the morning's announcements.
Oh god, y'all! The girl confided

to her nerdy but upstanding cohort,
(this wasn't technically inaccurate)

I was there that night! I was there!

from *Ploughshares*

Dog Tags

◇ ◇ ◇

Of us there is
      always less.
The days hammer

past, artificial daisies
      at the grave.
Words I didn't choose

for my father's headstone
      & those that came instead
to live around my neck,

dog tags a tin
      pendulum on my chest.
On my mother's side,

my cousin, too young,
      dirt a pile above her
but no stone, nothing

but the tinfoil name
      from the funeral home—
the fresh plastic

flowers that still wilt
      in this heat.
At blackjack

she lost
        everything my great-
aunt & -uncle had saved,

even their low ranch
        where I first
knew blue glass, plastic

covering the rug
        & the good couch
in the sitting room

no one dared sit.
        The prickly underside
of the clear runner a cactus

you couldn't help
        but touch. Uncle Wilmer's
pickup long paid off

now stares empty
        under somebody
else's tree. The liars

& book-cookers
        came with their knives
offering her

seconds, & she
        sat & ate—
once you've tasted

the stone-filled fruit
        of the underworld
you may never return.

They took everything
        from her
my mother says, both

of us shaking
           our heads, disbelieving
how exacting

death is, how deep
           the shade—
except breath.

She was in debt
           & dead within
a year, went through money

like water—
           And that didn't
last long either.

                from *Ploughshares*

CONTRIBUTORS' NOTES AND COMMENTS

ROSA ALCALÁ was born in Paterson, New Jersey, in 1969. She is the author of three books of poetry, most recently *MyOTHER TONGUE* (Futurepoem, 2017). The recipient of a National Endowment for the Arts Translation Fellowship, she is the editor and cotranslator of *New & Selected Poems of Cecilia Vicuña* (Kelsey Street Press, 2018). Her work was chosen for *The Best American Poetry 2019*. She is a professor of creative writing at the University of Texas at El Paso, and teaches in its Bilingual MFA Program.

Of "The Pyramid Scheme," Alcalá writes: "I can't help but think of the devastating impact that COVID-19 has had on nursing homes, although this poem was written long before the pandemic began. I am haunted by the image of someone like my mother, confined to a room, unable to visit with loved ones except through a window. Someone like my mother, dying alone. I think, too, about the underpaid and overworked nurses and aides who took care of my mother, who spoke to her in Spanish, and therefore grounded her, who brought her the food she liked when they thought she was getting too thin. My mother died a few years ago, but do her caretakers continue on under these terrible circumstances? Do they fear for their own lives but have no choice but go to work? I think of my aunt, who died during the pandemic, two decades after she was diagnosed with Alzheimer's, and who lived for many years in a nursing home. Whose funeral I watched on YouTube, because only her children were allowed at the service. What I mean to say is that the anger I express in this poem, directed mainly at a system that privileges some bodies above others, that does not care about the sick and the elderly, has not 'mellowed.' COVID-19 has simply exposed what was already broken."

LAUREN K. ALLEYNE was born in 1979 and raised in Trinidad and Tobago. She is the author of two collections of poetry, *Difficult Fruit*

(Peepal Tree Press, 2014) and *Honeyfish* (New Issues & Peepal Tree, 2019), and coeditor of *Furious Flower: Seeding the Future of African American Poetry* (Northwestern, 2020). She lives in Harrisonburg, Virginia, where she is an associate professor of English at James Madison University, and the assistant director of the Furious Flower Poetry Center. More information is available at www.laurenkalleyne.com.

Of "Divination," Alleyne writes: "In general, I am fascinated by the fact and idea of 'remains' and the way we can use them to read backward, gleaning information about a life. However, I encountered these remains in a workshop setting, as a prompt, and in that context, without any connection to the creature in its 'before,' I was surprised to find that I was less interested in what it had been than what it was becoming, and the strange journey this body was having. It struck me that remains are also the weird afterlife of the body itself, rather than just testimony of a prior life. The poem seeks, I think, to capture that train of thought."

JABARI ASIM was born in St. Louis, Missouri, in 1962. He writes poetry (*Stop and Frisk*); fiction (*A Taste of Honey*, *Only The Strong* [all from Bloomsday] and the forthcoming *Yonder*); nonfiction (*The N Word*, *We Can't Breathe*); and children's books, including *Preaching to the Chickens* and *A Child's Introduction to African American History*. He directs the MFA program in creative writing at Emerson College.

Of "Some Call It God," Asim writes: "In working toward a constructive disruption of my idea of the Divine, I'm embracing the notion of God as Funk, an irresistible impulse to drop everything and *move*. I can think of few experiences holier than responding to rhythm, whether it's coming from the beat of a drum or a church matron humming her favorite hymn."

JOSHUA BENNETT is the Mellon Assistant Professor of English and creative writing at Dartmouth. His three books of poetry and criticism are *The Sobbing School* (Penguin, 2016), winner of the National Poetry Series; *Being Property Once Myself* (Harvard University Press, 2020); and *Owed* (Penguin, 2020). Bennett earned his PhD in English from Princeton University, and an MA in Theatre and Performance Studies from the University of Warwick, where he was a Marshall Scholar. He has received fellowships from the National Endowment for the Arts, the Ford Foundation, MIT, and the Society of Fellows at Harvard University. His first work of narrative nonfiction, *Spoken Word: A Cultural History*, is forthcoming from Knopf.

Bennett writes: "I wrote 'Benediction' back when I lived in New York City. Rereading the poem now, I'm reminded of everything I love about that place. Uptown in particular. Harlem and Washington Heights, all that those neighborhoods taught me from the time I was a small boy about what it meant to do one's best to live and die with dignity. The poem is part of a sequence that is at the core of a new book I'm writing about black disposability, ecological catastrophe, and fatherhood. It recalls a world before the pandemic. It gestures toward the one we are building together, even now, in the midst of it. And the future world already on its way."

Born in 1981 and raised in Shreveport, Louisiana, DESTINY O. BIRD-SONG is a poet, essayist, and fiction writer who lives and works in Nashville, Tennessee. Her debut poetry collection, *Negotiations*, was published by Tin House Books in October 2020, and her debut novel is forthcoming from Grand Central in 2022. Her work has received support from Cave Canem, Callaloo, Jack Jones Literary Arts, Pink Door, MacDowell, the Ragdale Foundation, and the Tin House Summer Workshop.

Of "love poem that ends at popeyes," Birdsong writes: "I believe I write best about the transformative power of love when I'm narrating from a hopeless place, and this poem is one such instance. It was Valentine's Day 2018, and I was the sickest and the saddest I'd been in a long time. I was lying in bed trying to make myself comfortable, but I was also hungry and didn't want to go out for food, so I decided to write about what I craved. I also really wanted to write a poem where I indulged my most pitiful, maudlin sentiments about loneliness, but it ultimately turned into an exploration of desire, failed/found tenderness, self-detachment from infatuation/objectification, and of course, hope. It's one of those poems that read me as I wrote it. And although I knew how it would end before I began, I didn't know that writing it would make me feel a little less pitiful, a little more loved, and a little more satisfied with being alone.

"With regard to form, I settled on it in part because the poem was originally a block of text I'd typed into my phone, and someone in a workshop warned that journals might not publish it because it was too long. Since I don't believe in editing work solely for publication, breaking up the text seemed like a nice compromise. In hindsight, I love how the lines look randomly cast on the page like sacred lots, which directly relates to the speaker's ambivalence about finding love versus being satisfied with the 'enoughness' of her current situation.

Happiness is attainable, even though the future is uncertain and the present feels unbearable. And goodness, if I write poetry for any concrete, articulable reason, this might be it."

SUSAN BRIANTE was born in Newark, New Jersey, in 1967 and is the author most recently of *Defacing the Monument* (Noemi Press, 2020), a series of essays on immigration, archives, aesthetics, and the state. She has published three books of poetry: *Pioneers in the Study of Motion* (2007), *Utopia Minus* (2011), and *The Market Wonders* (2016), all from Ahsahta Press. Briante is a professor of creative writing at the University of Arizona.

Briante writes: "I wrote 'Further Exercises' as I finished work on my book *Defacing the Monument*, a series of essays that (among other things) tries to think through the ethics of writing about crisis. While writing can transform readers and shift perceptions, I felt haunted by the limits of what it can do. The poem was a way to trace that uneasiness."

JERICHO BROWN was born in Shreveport, Louisiana, in 1976. He is the author of *The Tradition* (Copper Canyon Press, 2019), which won the Pulitzer Prize. His first book, *Please* (New Issues, 2008), won the American Book Award. His second book, *The New Testament* (Copper Canyon, 2014), won the Anisfield-Wolf Book Award. *The Tradition* also won the Paterson Poetry Prize. Brown is the director of the creative writing program and the Charles Howard Candler Professor of English at Emory University.

Brown writes: " 'Work' is the result of my having been commissioned to write a poem in response to the 2019–2020 Romare Bearden exhibit at the High Museum in Atlanta, Georgia, where I live."

CHRISTOPHER BUCKLEY was born in Arcata, California, in 1948, and grew up in Santa Barbara. He taught at Fresno State and the University of California, Santa Barbara and Riverside. Recent books of poetry are *Star Journal: Selected Poems* (University of Pittsburgh Press, 2016), *Chaos Theory* (Plume Editions, 2018), *Cloud Memoir: Selected Longer Poems 1987–2017* (Stephen F. Austin State University Press, 2018), *Agnostic* (Lynx House Press, 2019), and *The Pre-Eternity of the World* (Stephen F. Austin, 2021). He has edited several critical collections and anthologies, most recently *The Long Embrace: Contemporary Poets on the Long Poems of Philip Levine* (Lynx House Press, 2020) and *Naming the Lost: The Fresno Poets—Interviews and Essays* (Stephen F. Austin,

2021). Buckley was a Guggenheim Fellow in Poetry for 2007–2008. He received the 2008 James Dickey Prize from *Five Points* magazine, a Fulbright Award in Creative Writing to the former Yugoslavia, four Pushcart Prizes, two awards from the Poetry Society of America, and NEA grants in poetry for 2001 and 1984.

Of "After Tu Fu," Buckley writes: "Certainly I am not alone in revering and drawing inspiration from Tu Fu. Many years ago an opening line of one of his poems set me off, something close to the opening here about facing the winter dawn. I was thinking of January and an upcoming birthday, and as always about the passing of time. Not much original there. But the voice in Tu Fu's poem centered the emotion and set a response to experience going for me—his honesty and clarity, the modesty in the face of change, the managing of nostalgia and cherishing of life. The poem saw many iterations, beginning as a prose piece. Then over the years, several versions, until this final distillation. For me, art is always long, and it took many rewrites over the years to arrive at this final form."

VICTORIA CHANG was born in Detroit, Michigan, in 1970. Her most recent poetry book is *OBIT*, published by Copper Canyon Press in 2020. She has published four other poetry books, of which the most recent prior book is *Barbie Chang* (Copper Canyon, 2017). A book of hybrid essays called *Dear Memory* is forthcoming from Milkweed Editions in 2021. A new book of poems, *The Trees Witness Everything*, is forthcoming from Copper Canyon in 2022. She also occasionally writes children's books, of which the most recent is a middle-grade verse novel, *Love, Love* (Sterling Publishing, 2020). She lives in Los Angeles and is the program chair of Antioch's MFA program in creative writing.

Chang writes: "I wrote this 'Marfa, Texas' poem during a Lannan Residency Fellowship. At the time, I wasn't writing poems and hadn't written a poem in so long (maybe five years) that I wasn't sure I would ever write a poem again. I had planned to take long walks, look at art objects, and read instead. But a friend who was in residence at the MacDowell Colony at the same time started writing poem letters to me so that I might start writing again. I initially resisted, but soon began to enjoy writing again. This poem was one of those poem letters that I wrote back to my friend. I'm grateful, as when I returned home, I began writing many more poems. This one's shape was inspired by the art objects I viewed at the Judd Foundation and the Chinati Foundation."

CHEN CHEN was born in Xiamen, China, in 1989. He is the author of *When I Grow Up I Want to Be a List of Further Possibilities* (BOA Editions, 2017), which was nominated for the National Book Award for Poetry and won the Thom Gunn Award for Gay Poetry. He has received a Pushcart Prize and a fellowship from the National Endowment for the Arts. He teaches at Brandeis University.

Of "The School of Eternities," Chen writes: "This is a love poem and also an ode to Wegmans, a supermarket chain I first encountered while living in Syracuse, New York. I didn't understand why so many people I met in Syracuse talked so much about this supermarket. Over time I came to see how it was a cultural phenomenon that united people, that provided a sense of identity and geography; Wegmans as a beacon, as one of the cardinal directions! There's north, south, east, west, and Wegmans. For years I associated the supermarket with upstate New York, as well as with my partner, who was born and raised in that region. Falling in love with a person can also make you fall in love with a place. Moving across the country to Lubbock, Texas, for the creative writing PhD program at Texas Tech meant no more Wegmans. And I thought moving back to where I grew up, in the Boston area, would mean that, too—when in fact, we now live twenty minutes' driving distance from a two-story, very fancy Wegmans. However trivial and sentimental, it's been a source of comfort, especially during this era of the coronavirus pandemic. In its later movement, this poem is an elegy for my partner's mother, who died in 2015 from pancreatic cancer. She also loved talking about trips to Wegmans. So it doesn't strike me as at all odd for this piece to be simultaneously a love poem, an elegy, and an ode to a supermarket."

Born in South Korea in 1992 and raised mainly in Indiana, SU CHO earned her BA from Emory University and her MFA in Poetry from Indiana University. Her essay "Cleaving Translation" won *The Sycamore Review*'s nonfiction prize. She lives in Milwaukee and is pursuing a PhD. You can find her at suchowrites.com.

Cho writes: "Before my family immigrated to Queens, New York, I was equipped with my hot pink Barbie traveling house suitcase and the ABCs. I felt unstoppable. I must have been hopeful, though I did not know that word, because I believed that if I knew 'dog' and 'cat,' I would be okay. I quickly learned that was not true.

" 'Abecedarian for ESL in West Lafayette, Indiana' is a rare poem for me because it found the page quickly, and I feel as though I wrote the poem just for myself. The abecedarian guided me in a way that sometimes felt effortless but was quick to remind me that the notion of effortlessness requires a lot of foundational work. I often say that my memory of speaking Korean is entangled with my memory of learning English. My ability to speak the language is not a given because it took a lot of work from my parents, memories both good and bad. This poem was a way for me to remember and perhaps for others to remember. I remember the sounds of Korean words before I can remember what those sounds mean, and I'll run through what sounds right to me until my parents say yes, ok, that one, we know what you mean. This poem marks the unremarkable wrongs of childhood. But I wrote them down to remember because if not for them, how would I recognize my feelings and rage today?"

AMA CODJOE was born in Austin, Texas, in 1979 and was raised in Youngstown, Ohio. She is the author of *Bluest Nude* (Milkweed Editions, forthcoming in 2022) and *Blood of the Air* (Northwestern University Press, 2020), winner of the Drinking Gourd Chapbook Poetry Prize. She has received a 2017 Rona Jaffe Writer's Award, a 2019 Creative Writing Fellowship from the National Endowment for the Arts, a 2020 NYSCA/NYFA Artist Fellowship, and a 2021 Jerome Hill Artist Fellowship.

HENRI COLE was born in Fukuoka, Japan, in 1956. He has published ten collections of poetry, including *Middle Earth* (Farrar, Straus and Giroux, 2003). He has received the Jackson Prize, the Kingsley Tufts Award, the Rome Prize, the Berlin Prize, the Lenore Marshall Award, and the Medal in Poetry from the American Academy of Arts and Letters. His most recent collection is *Blizzard* (FSG, 2020). A memoir, *Orphic Paris*, was published by New York Review Books in 2018. He teaches at Claremont McKenna College and lives in Boston.

Cole writes: "'Gross National Unhappiness' appears in my collection *Blizzard* after the poem 'Super Bloom,' in which I say, 'You said you would always / tell the truth, Mr. President, but that was a lie, so I'm / pressing my white face to your White House door.' 'Gross National Unhappiness' is a postscript. I am not sure if it is civic, or ethical, or political. As a history poem with a singular self, it remembers Lowell, Rich, and McKay. It uses anaphora and aphorism, two of my favorite devices. Though the theme is dark, I want the title to give a little chuckle. Though I live quietly, I write, in part, to decry the abuse of power, and to uplift 'vagrants, self-haters, hermits, junkies, / chumps, the defeated, the paranoid, / the penniless, and those led astray by desire.' "

BILLY COLLINS was born in the French Hospital in New York City in 1941. He was an undergraduate at Holy Cross College and received his Ph.D. from the University of California, Riverside. His books of poetry include *Whale Day* (Random House, 2020), *The Rain in Portugal* (Random House, 2016), *Aimless Love: New and Selected Poems 2003–2013* (Random House, 2013), *Horoscopes for the Dead* (Random House, 2011), *Ballistics* (Random House, 2008), *The Trouble With Poetry and Other Poems* (Random House, 2005), a collection of haiku titled *She Was Just Seventeen* (Modern Haiku Press, 2006), *Nine Horses* (Random House, 2002), *Sailing Alone Around the Room: New and Selected Poems* (Random House, 2001), *Picnic, Lightning* (University of Pittsburgh Press, 1998), *The Art of Drowning* (University of Pittsburgh Press, 1995), and *Questions About Angels* (William Morrow, 1991), which was selected for the National Poetry Series by Edward Hirsch and reprinted by the University of Pittsburgh Press in 1999. He is the editor of *Poetry 180: A Turning Back to Poetry* (Random House, 2003) and *180 More: Extraordinary Poems for Everyday* (Random House, 2005). He is a former Distinguished Professor of English at Lehman College (City University of New York). A frequent contributor and former guest editor of *The Best American Poetry* series, he was appointed United States Poet Laureate 2001–2003 and served as New York State Poet 2004–2006. He also edited *Bright Wings: An Anthology of Poems about Birds* illustrated by David Sibley (Columbia University Press, 2010). He was recently inducted into the American Academy of Arts and Letters.

Of "On the Deaths of Friends," Collins writes: "I think this poem can happily explain itself on the page, but I can say something about its progress and its sources. It begins by weaving through some popular sequences of dying, then oddly switches to the tone of a lecturer ('will not be considered here'). The speaker is now abruptly placed by a lakefront at evening, momentarily giving the poem the stability of a time and a place. Here, the speaker falls into a meditation (greater Romantic lyric), in which he tries to imagine where his deceased friends have gone (*In Memoriam*), a 'place' far removed from the joys of life (fox, kettle). He runs along a train platform like a man in a black-and-white movie, before returning to the present and the sensorium where he began (ripples, breeze, whistle, trees, clouds), only now he is left shiv-

ering in the face of his own mortality and overwhelmed by the power-
ful inflowing of perception."

ADAM O. DAVIS was born in Tucson, Arizona, in 1980, and raised in
France, New Jersey, Scotland, and Utah. He is the author of *Index
of Haunted Houses* (Sarabande, 2020), winner of the Kathryn A. Mor-
ton Poetry Prize. The recipient of the 2016 George Bogin Memorial
Award from the Poetry Society of America, he lives in San Diego, Cal-
ifornia, where he teaches English literature at The Bishop's School.

Davis writes: "The earliest iteration of 'Interstate Highway System'
served as a series of terse second-person commands—something of
a lyric roadmap telling you to go this way, then that, now this until
you arrived at the poem's ultimate question, which is, of course: How
will you live with and within yourself under the umbrella of Amer-
ica? I don't know much better now than I did then, but subsequent
drafts expanded the telegraphic directions and shifted the focus inward
so that 'I' now had to answer for what was being offered. That, cou-
pled with a peripatetic life and roughly 3,000 miles' worth of roadside
observations gleaned from a 2015 road trip following defunct railroad
lines from Pittsburgh to San Diego (a story for another time), soon
brought the poem as it is now known into being, though I'm indebted
to Jericho Brown who turned it down the first time I submitted it to
The Believer, noting that it was close but the ending needed some work
and I should resend it when the work was done. When the work was
done I did exactly that and I must've done something right because not
only did he publish it but it's now published here."

KWAME DAWES was born in 1962 in Accra, Ghana, and raised in
Jamaica. He is the author of twenty-two books of poetry and numer-
ous other books of fiction, criticism, and essays. His latest collection,
Nebraska, was published in 2020. He is Glenna Luschei Editor of *Prai-
rie Schooner* and teaches at the University of Nebraska and the Pacific
MFA Program. He is director of the African Poetry Book Fund and
artistic director of the Calabash International Literary Festival. Dawes
is a Chancellor of the Academy of American Poets and a Fellow of the
Royal Society of Literature. He has won an Emmy, the Forward Poetry
Prize, a Guggenheim Fellowship, and the Windham Campbell Prize
for poetry. In 2021, Kwame Dawes was named editor of "American
Life in Poetry" column.

Of "Before the Riot," Dawes writes: "Sometime close to writing this poem, meaning, in May 2020, I also wrote, 'We who live inside / history go blind to its machinations; / and this is the use of poetry.' Which is to say that my hope is that poetry is resistant to this blindness—not a blessing, really, but a necessity. This year, I have felt acutely this sense of living inside history."

Toi Derricotte was born in Detroit, Michigan, in 1941. Her sixth collection of poetry, *"I": New and Selected Poems*, was published in 2019. Other books of poetry include *The Undertaker's Daughter, Tender*, and *Captivity*. Her literary memoir, *The Black Notebooks*, received the Anisfield-Wolf Book Award for nonfiction and was a *New York Times* Notable Book of the Year. She was awarded the Frost Medal in 2020 and has received three Pushcart Prizes, the 2012 Paterson Poetry Prize for Sustained Literary Achievement, a Distinguished Pioneering of the Arts Award from the United Black Artists, and the 2012 PEN/Voelcker Award for Poetry. With Cornelius Eady, she cofounded the Cave Canem Foundation, a home for the many voices of African American poetry. She is professor emerita from the University of Pittsburgh and a former Chancellor of the Academy of American Poets.

Derricotte writes: "The poem 'The Great Beauty' was written years after I saw the movie but just a few days after I saw the pigeons. I found myself one day at a Zoom meeting, talking about the appearance of the pigeons when I had been out walking, and the people who heard the story seemed to get a kick out of it. I'd never thought about translating a story about some event in my daily life into a poem. Usually I think daily events aren't worthy of poetry. However, since people seemed to enjoy the story, I thought, why not try? And I had promised a friend to exchange a new poem with her that very evening.

"When I sat down to write, I remembered the flamingos' appearance in the movie I had seen and I made the connection between the two events. And so 'The Great Beauty' was written."

Jay Deshpande was born in Austin, Texas, in 1984. He is the author of *Love the Stranger* (YesYes Books, 2015) and the chapbooks *The Rest of the Body* (YesYes Books, 2017) and *The Umbrian Sonnets* (PANK, 2020). He is the recipient of a Wallace Stegner fellowship, a Kundiman fellowship, the Scotti Merrill Memorial Award, and residencies at Civitella Ranieri and the Saltonstall Arts Colony. He teaches at Columbia University and in the Brooklyn Poets Mentorship Program.

Of "A Child's Guide to Grasses," Deshpande writes: "I grew up in rural New Hampshire, and much of my interior landscape is furnished by the woods and fields I played in as a child. But there's something solipsistic about childhood memory: you recall how things felt and smelled, but it is much harder to decipher context. When I think about growing up near Dartmouth College (motto: *Vox clamantis in deserto*), I want to recognize how power played out on the land. Exactly whose 'wilderness' was this? By exploring this question on the level of language and the sensorium, I began to consider how my childhood adjacent to academia shaped my relationship to institutions of power as an adult." *Editor's note*: the Dartmouth motto translates as "a voice crying from the wilderness."

NATALIE DIAZ was born in the Fort Mojave Indian Village in Needles, California. She is Mojave and Akimel O'odham. She has two books: *When My Brother Was an Aztec* (Copper Canyon Press, 2012) and *Postcolonial Love Poem* (Graywolf, 2020).

Of "lake-loop," Diaz writes: "This poem began as many of my poems do lately, in water, in desire, in wonder of my body in relationship to the body of land. When you say the word 'lake' in Mojave, you are saying that the lake is a body of water who is alone. I have been thinking about this loneliness for years. This wanting to return to the other body/bodies that are also yours, to want to be in relationship with, one of many, not the center but overwhelmed in momentum."

ALEX DIMITROV is the author of three books of poetry—*Love and Other Poems* (Copper Canyon Press, 2021), *Together and by Ourselves* (Copper Canyon, 2017), *Begging for It* (Four Way Books, 2013)—and the chapbook *American Boys* (Floating Wolf Quarterly, 2012). He has taught writing at Princeton University, Columbia University, and New York University, and was the senior content editor at the Academy of American Poets. Dimitrov founded the queer poetry salon Wilde Boys (2009–13), which brought together emerging and established writers in Manhattan's Greenwich Village. With Dorothea Lasky, he cofounded Astro Poets and is the coauthor of *Astro Poets: Your Guides to the Zodiac* (Flatiron Books, 2019). On Twitter, he writes an endless poem called "Love" in real time, one tweet a day. He was born in Sofia, Bulgaria, in 1984, and lives in New York City.

Of "Love," Dimitrov writes: "I wrote this poem, one line a day, throughout the Trump presidency. There seemed to be so much negativity everywhere—in the country, online, and even in art—that I wanted to remember what I loved about life. I wanted to give people hope."

RITA DOVE was born in Akron, Ohio, in 1952. She is the author of a novel, short stories, the drama *The Darker Face of the Earth*, as well as ten books of poetry, including *Thomas and Beulah*, winner of the 1987 Pulitzer Prize, and *Sonata Mulattica*, a poetic tribute to nineteenth century Afro-European violin prodigy George Bridgetower (2010 Hurston/Wright Legacy Award). Her eleventh poetry collection is *Playlist for the Apocalypse* (W. W. Norton, 2021). She has received an NAACP Image Award (for *Collected Poems 1974–2004*), the Heinz Award in the Arts and Humanities, and the Academy of American Poets' Wallace Stevens Award. She was U.S. Poet Laureate from 1993 to 1995 and is the only poet to have received both the National Humanities Medal (from President Clinton, 1996) and the National Medal of Arts (from President Obama, 2011). She edited *The Best American Poetry 2000* and *The Penguin Anthology of 20th-Century American Poetry*, and has written weekly poetry columns for both *The Washington Post* and *The New York Times*. A member of the American Academy of Arts and Sciences and the American Academy of Arts and Letters, Dove is Henry Hoyns Professor of Creative Writing at the University of Virginia, where she has been teaching since 1989.

Of "Naji, 14. Philadelphia.," Dove writes: "I usually have little recollection of a poem's origin story—partly because the path from first spark to completed text is often a long and fractured one, but also because each poem's trajectory is so different, trying to replicate past strategies would be futile. I do remember that this poem was initially one of a series of testimonials to Black Lives Matter, with each title consisting of a first name plus one distinguishing word. I had written the first poem ('Trayvon, Redux') just days after that tragedy in a red-hot rage; but as the tally grew—and with it the impunity granted to the perpetrators—so, too, did my despair, a kind of ferocious hopelessness. Who could have imagined such an escalation of racially tinged acts, each more outrageous and tragic and utterly senseless than the last? No words seemed able to encompass what was happening in our neighborhoods, in our country.

"By the time Naji's story hit the public, four years had passed since Trayvon Martin's murder. The number of Black victims to police brutality—intentional or accidental, undocumented or filmed or word against word, but nearly always defended by those in blue and justified by their political and judicial enablers—continued to mount. I worried that I had become numb to the steady barrage of hatred. And then suddenly—while reading a newspaper account I would have wished away if I could—very clearly I heard a fourteen-year-old boy asking for his mother, begging for a place to lay his head. I could not soothe him, so I let him speak.

"P.S.: After a week in the ICU, this young man survived—but I'm not sure about his childhood or his soul."

CAMILLE T. DUNGY, born in Colorado and raised in California, is the author of the essay collection *Guidebook to Relative Strangers: Journeys into Race, Motherhood, and History* (W. W. Norton, 2017) and four collections of poetry, most recently *Trophic Cascade* (Wesleyan, 2017). She edited *Black Nature: Four Centuries of African American Nature Poetry* (University of Georgia Press, 2009), coedited the *From the Fishouse* poetry anthology (Persea, 2009), and served as assistant editor on *Gathering Ground: Celebrating Cave Canem's First Decade* (University of Michigan Press, 2006). She is the poetry editor for *Orion Magazine*. She has been awarded a Guggenheim Fellowship, an American Book Award, a Colorado Book Award, two Northern California Book Awards, two NAACP Image Award Nominations, and fellowships from the NEA in both prose and poetry. Dungy is currently a University Distinguished Professor in the English department at Colorado State University. www.camilledungy.com

Dungy writes: "I wrote 'This'll hurt me more' during a spring/summer of protests in America, which could be any spring/summer in America, but which, in this case, was the spring/summer of 2020. I was exhausted when I wrote this poem. I'm still exhausted now."

LOUISE ERDRICH was born in Little Falls, Minnesota, in 1954. Her novels include *Love Medicine* (Harper & Row, 1984) and *LaRose* (HarperCollins, 2012), both winners of the National Book Critics Circle Prize for Fiction, *The Plague of Doves* (HarperCollins, 2006), and *The Round House* (HarperCollins, 2014), which received the National Book Award. Her last book of poetry was *Original Fire* (HarperCollins, 2003). She lives in Minnesota and is the owner of a small independent bookstore, Birchbark Books.

Of "Stone Love," Erdrich writes: "I was driving my daughter and her friend back from a summer camp for Native students at the University of Iowa. They were asleep in the backseat. I was thinking about meteors and a lusciously curved stone bench that a friend of mine was making. Words surged into my mind and at the same time a thunderstorm hit and there was nowhere to stop. I could hardly see through the rain. Lightning was crackling down all around us. Still, lines and words kept arriving. It was very inconvenient, but what an experience. . . . I finally pulled off at a fast-food place, sent the girls inside, and wrote the poem on an unpaid parking ticket."

KATHY FAGAN's fifth book, *Sycamore* (Milkweed, 2017), was a finalist for the 2018 Kingsley Tufts Award. Milkweed will publish her new collection, *Bad Hobby*, in 2022. Born in New York in 1958, Fagan has received fellowships from the NEA, the Ingram Merrill Foundation, and the Ohio Arts Council. She directs the MFA program at The Ohio State University in Columbus, Ohio, where she also serves as series coeditor for the OSU Press/*The Journal* Wheeler Poetry Prize. This is her first appearance in *The Best American Poetry*.

Of "Conqueror," Fagan writes: "When my deaf, dementing dad lived with me, I planned each day around his care. Caregivers know just how intense rare moments of freedom can feel; some may experience a keener sense of time and its passing. Those years are mostly over for me now, but what I learned about the dynamics of our little family, as well as larger American institutions failing the poor, the aged, and the disabled every day, has informed my later life and work irrevocably."

CHANDA FELDMAN was born in Knoxville, Tennessee, in 1976. She is the author of *Approaching the Fields* (LSU Press, 2018) and is an assistant professor of creative writing at Oberlin College.

Of "They Ran and Flew from You," Feldman writes: "This poem is based on the walks I took with my kids to and after school when we lived in central Israel. I was mesmerized to witness how they maneuvered in their surroundings, to see what they were clued into that I, as an immigrant, was not: they knew the wild plants they could eat and the ones not to touch, and they were always teaching me Hebrew rhymes, poems, and songs. There was also the pleasure of observing my kids' continual and evolving games with their friends on the park structures they visited every day. Watching these daily scenes, I was reminded how place imprints us and structures our knowledge and memories."

NIKKY FINNEY was born by the sea in South Carolina in 1957 and raised during the Civil Rights, Black Power, and Black Arts Movements. She is the author of *On Wings Made of Gauze* (Morrow, 1985), *Rice* (TriQuarterly, reprinted in 2013), *The World Is Round* (TriQuarterly, reprinted in 2013), and *Head Off & Split* (TriQuarterly, 2011), which won the National Book Award for Poetry. Her new collection of poems, *Love Child's Hotbed of Occasional Poetry*, was released from TriQuarterly Books/Northwestern University Press in 2020.

Of "I Feel Good," Finney writes: "Growing up in South Carolina in the 1970s meant that James Brown was always singing truth and dance music in my ear. His music raised me and raised my Black consciousness, too. When I heard that the money he left in his will to the 'needy children of South Carolina and Georgia' never made it to them but instead was being gobbled up by rich white lawyers who didn't think a Black man could make such a rich decision on his own—about where his hard earned money should go—I wanted to write something for him—and for the hundreds of other Black musicians whose money was posthumously preyed over by men who couldn't even dance."

LOUISE GLÜCK was born in New York City in 1943. Among many honors for her work are a 1993 Pulitzer Prize for *The Wild Iris*, a 2014 National Book Award for *Faithful and Virtuous Night*, and the Nobel Prize for Literature in 2020. She teaches at Yale University and Stanford University, and was the guest editor of *The Best American Poetry 1993*.

NANCY MILLER GOMEZ was born in Greenwich, Connecticut, but grew up in Kansas. She worked in Los Angeles as a lawyer and a television producer before moving to Santa Cruz, California. She cofounded the Santa Cruz Poetry Project to provide poetry workshops to incarcerated men and women. Her chapbook, *Punishment*, was published in 2018 as part of the Rattle chapbook series. She has an MFA from Pacific University and is working on her first full-length manuscript.

Of "Tilt-A-Whirl," Gomez writes: "The Kansas I grew up in was a land of contradictions: wholesome and quaint with an undercurrent of squalor. But the weird Americana of my childhood has provided a wellspring of material: pig farmers, livery barns, truck stops, horse traders. My older sister Janis chauffeured me through the rural Midwest of my youth. In summer, we traversed the back roads of Kansas and Missouri, blasting Pink Floyd in an old Skylark with the windows down. Once we stopped at a small town carnival on a weekday. Despite its cheerful facade, an empty carnival is a haunted, unhappy place. Against this backdrop, I witnessed for the first time how my beautiful sister attracted attention from men in a way that felt dangerous. It was a revelation made all the more impactful because I idolized her. To me, she was mature, worldly, and in control, so to see her made defenseless was terrifying. In retrospect, I recognize she was only sixteen at the time, still a child despite her self-assured way of moving through the world. But the feeling of being caught on the wrong side of a power imbalance has stayed with me all these years and resurfaced in this poem."

JORIE GRAHAM was born in New York City in 1950 and raised in Italy. She returned to the United States to finish her education. Her fourteen collections of poetry include, recently, *Fast* and *Runaway*, both from HarperCollins/Ecco. Two volumes of her selected poetry have appeared: *The Dream of the Unified Field*, which was awarded the Pulitzer Prize in 1996, and *From the New World*. Graham was the guest editor of *The Best American Poetry 1990*. She lives in Massachusetts and teaches at Harvard University.

RACHEL ELIZA GRIFFITHS is a poet, novelist, and visual artist. Her most recent collection, a hybrid of poetry and photography, is *Seeing the Body* (W. W. Norton 2020), which was nominated for a 2021 NAACP Image Award. Griffiths has received fellowships from Kimbilio, Cave Canem Foundation, Robert Rauschenberg Foundation, and Yaddo. Her debut novel, *Promise*, is forthcoming from Random House in 2022. She lives in New York City.

FRANCINE J. HARRIS was born in Detroit, Michigan, in 1972. She is the author of three collections of poetry: *Here is the Sweet Hand* (Farrar, Straus and Giroux, 2020), *play dead* (Alice James Books, 2016), and *allegiance* (Wayne State University Press, 2012). *play dead* was the winner of the Lambda Literary and Audre Lorde Awards. An associate professor of English at the University of Houston, she has received fellowships from the National Endowment for the Arts, the MacDowell Colony, and the Cullman Center for Scholars and Writers at the New York Public Library.

Of "Sonata in F Minor, K.183: Allegro," Harris writes: "In addition to the ekphrastic tribute, I love being able to connect my work to Ann

Petry's seminal novel. Reading *The Street* during my brief return to New York was rather uncanny. So much paranoia haunts this cautionary tale that it is difficult to parse from actual danger; and thus spoke to much of the experience I was having this time around with the city—the bustle, the crowds, the rush. Everything seemed to blur into a haze of possible disaster—which may be bad for stress level, but great for poems!"

TERRANCE HAYES was born in Columbia, South Carolina, in 1971. His most recent publications include *American Sonnets for My Past and Future Assassin* (Penguin, 2018), and *To Float in the Space Between: A Life and Work in Conversation with the Life and Work of Etheridge Knight* (Wave Books, 2018). He was the guest editor of *The Best American Poetry 2014*.

Of "George Floyd," Hayes writes: "I heard the protesters marching by my home that first Friday after George Floyd was murdered. I left my desk to walk with them into Washington Square Park. All of it was peaceful. All of it cathartic. When we stood in the park there were these blue spells of silence between chants. I went home and wrote this poem."

EDWARD HIRSCH was born in Chicago, Illinois, in 1950 and educated at Grinnell College and the University of Pennsylvania. He has published ten books of poems, including *Gabriel: A Poem* (Alfred A. Knopf, 2014), a book-length elegy for his son, and *Stranger by Night* (Alfred A. Knopf, 2020). He has also published six prose books, most recently *A Poet's Glossary* (Houghton Mifflin Harcourt, 2014), a full compendium of poetic terms, and *100 Poems to Break Your Heart* (Houghton Mifflin Harcourt, 2021). He was the guest editor of *The Best American Poetry 2016*. He is a MacArthur Fellow and serves as president of the John Simon Guggenheim Memorial Foundation.

Of "Waste Management," Hirsch writes: "It was a sort of schooling—that job as a garbageman in my hometown. It was an experience that changed me. The poem is directive and addresses my twenty-year-old self in the present tense—do this, but don't do that—in one run-on onrushing sentence of short, jittery lines that tries to capture a working day on the route, my formal education in collecting trash, finding out what it means to work for a living, getting a hard daily lesson in becoming invisible."

ISHION HUTCHINSON was born in Port Antonio, Jamaica. He is the author of the poetry collections *Far District* (Peepal Tree Press, 2010) and *House of Lords and Commons* (Farrar, Straus and Giroux, 2016), which won the National Book Critics Circle Award.

Of "David," Hutchinson writes: "The poem's shape, unlikely as it may seem, is a madrigal in the sense that it counterpoints various fictive moments of incoherence out of twice standing, both times speechless, in front of Michelangelo's *David*. The first encounter solidifies what Derek Walcott calls poetry, the combination of the natural and the marmoreal. The second encounter is more disturbing: David is both agent and witness to the horror of history which is the future of the giant's fall, a catastrophe he is powerless to change. God has compromised David; the imminent victory will be a false victory, and what will remain for David, and for us, is the struggle to regain free will over divine will. Still, after such knowledge, what innocence? The poem wants to know."

DIDI JACKSON, born in Columbus, Ohio, is the author of *Moon Jar* (Red Hen Press, 2020). Her work has appeared in *The New Yorker*, *The Kenyon Review*, *New England Review*, and *Ploughshares*. She teaches creative writing at Vanderbilt University.

Of "Two Mule Deer," Jackson writes: "When I was at the Montalvo Arts Center in Saratoga, California (as a guest/partner), I sat looking out a wall of windows in our studio as two female mule deer emerged from the surrounding woods and passed right by me. It was Jennifer Johns who said that deer are good determiners of danger. She knew I was afraid of hiking with the possibility of mountain lions nearby, especially since a man was killed by a mountain lion while biking earlier that month. The lines 'You know how it feels / wanting to walk into / the rain and disappear' are from Mary Oliver's poem 'At Blackwater Pond' in her book *Twelve Moons*. I hope this poem might bring attention to issues of sexual assault."

MAJOR JACKSON is the author of five books of poetry, most recently *The Absurd Man* (W. W. Norton, 2020) and *Roll Deep* (Norton, 2016). Recipient of fellowships from the John Simon Guggenheim Foundation and National Endowment for the Arts, he is the Gertrude Conaway Vanderbilt Professor of English at Vanderbilt University. He is the poetry editor of the *Harvard Review* and was the guest editor of *The Best American Poetry 2019*.

Of "Double Major," Jackson writes: "Since encountering W. E. B. DuBois's notion of 'double-consciousness,' I have long contemplated the phenomenon of the divided self and the authenticating act of poetry as a means of bringing into conversation those contained multitudes. In this case, in writing the poem I was also instinctively hunting down a relationship between freedom and the unconscious, how my lifelong pursuit for language has ultimately been about a quest for individuation, emotional and intellectual clarity, and salvation. This self-portrait poem, like others written in this vein, is indebted to Jorge Luis Borges, and has allowed me to give form to that interplay between my psychic landscapes and the other Majors who show up when I sit down to write."

AMAUD JAMAUL JOHNSON was born in Compton, California, in 1972. He is the author of three poetry collections, *Imperial Liquor* (University of Pittsburgh Press, 2020), *Darktown Follies* (Tupelo Press, 2013), and *Red Summer* (Tupelo Press, 2006). He has received a Pushcart Prize, the Hurston/Wright Legacy Award, the Edna Meudt Poetry Award, and the Dorset Prize, as well as fellowships from MacDowell, Stanford, Bread Loaf, and Cave Canem. He directs the MFA program in creative writing at the University of Wisconsin-Madison, where he is the Halls Bascom Professor of English.

Of "So Much for America," Johnson writes: "The last time I was handcuffed, I lived in Washington, DC. I was walking home from the post office, and a patrol car cut me off on the sidewalk. Someone had robbed a convenience store a few blocks away. One of the police officers almost jumped, Starsky and Hutch style, over the hood to approach me. I don't remember being afraid, but I felt cold. This was routine. I felt absent from my body, like I was looking down at myself, or watching a film. They threw me in the back of a car, then in a lineup of 'suspects' on the street in front of a bank near Dupont Circle. I didn't cry until the detective called me a liar. I had so many eyes on me. I just stood there waiting. I think I'm still waiting."

YUSEF KOMUNYAKAA was born in Bogalusa, Louisiana, in 1947. His most recent collection, *Everyday Mojo Songs of Earth: New and Selected Poems*, was published by Farrar, Straus and Giroux in 2021. He was the guest editor of *The Best American Poetry 2003*. He recently retired from teaching in the creative writing program at New York University.

Komunyakaa writes: "'Wheelchair' is a poem that splits in halves. The first sentence divides into four tercets: After my stroke on January 7, 2018, for weeks I was wheeled to therapy sessions; then I began wheeling myself. For one who loved to walk great distances, to endure physical tasks, I was grateful for the wheelchair—but also ready to arm myself with a cane or walker. The second sentence was almost given to me. I remember my maternal grandmother, Mary Washington, telling me about her mother who had rheumatism so extreme that her legs curled under her, but she would sit in her wheelchair and work in her garden for hours. I never knew my great-grandma, but I can still hear Mama Mary telling me the details. Perhaps we must also be good listeners."

DANA LEVIN was born in Los Angeles, California, in 1965 and grew up in the Mojave Desert. She is the author of four books of poetry, most recently *Banana Palace* (Copper Canyon Press, 2016) and *Sky Burial* (Copper Canyon, 2011), which *The New Yorker* called "utterly her own and utterly riveting." Levin is a grateful recipient of many fellowships and awards, including those from the Rona Jaffe, Whiting, and Guggenheim Foundations. She serves as Distinguished Writer in Residence at Maryville University in Saint Louis. Copper Canyon will publish her fifth book, *Now Do You Know Where You Are*, in 2022.

Of "Immigrant Song," Levin writes: "More than fifteen years ago, the poem arrived as a foreigner. While it offered an origin story of sorts for my maternal grandparents, their children, and myself as strangers in America, I did not understand why the poem had come when it did: in terms of subject and style, it was unlike anything else I was working on. I put it aside and forgot about it. Then a few years ago, while trawling for material, I found it in a file called 'The Abandoned'—and was surprised to find it had other poems, recent ones, to talk to: they spoke the same language, and circled the same subjects: inclusion, exclusion, prejudice, identity, choice. What is it to be an outsider, both in the nation and in the family, in the world and in the mind?"

ADA LIMÓN was born in 1976 in Sonoma, California. She is the author of five books of poetry, including *The Carrying* (Milkweed, 2018), which won the National Book Critics Circle Award. Her fourth book, *Bright Dead Things*, was published by Milkweed in 2015.

Of "The End of Poetry" Limón writes: "When the pandemic began, there was so much silence and anxiety that I found myself unable to read and write. I was very aware of the way language fails us, how poetry fails us, even when it saves us, too. Poems and their subjects felt almost pointless against the great grief of the world. This poem came out of that surrender. I had given up on words and then, of course, they came and brought me back to life."

JAMES LONGENBACH was born in Plainfield, New Jersey, in 1959. A poet and literary critic, he is the author most recently of the poetry collections *Forever* (W. W. Norton, 2021) and *Earthling* (Norton, 2017). His books of criticism include *The Lyric Now* (University of Chicago Press, 2020) and *How Poems Get Made* (Norton, 2018). The recipient of awards from the American Academy of Arts and Letters, the Guggenheim Foundation, and the Mellon Foundation, he is Joseph Gilmore Professor of English at the University of Rochester. He has also taught at the Bread Loaf Writers' Conference, Oxford University, Princeton University, and the Warren Wilson MFA Program for Writers.

Of "In the Village," Longenbach writes: "As a teenager, I assembled a copy of a seventeenth-century Flemish harpsichord, the parts milled by Zuckermann Harpsichords in the seaside village of Stonington, Connecticut. I then read the poems of James Merrill, who lived in that village until his death in 1995. Recently, 'In the Village' came to me while my wife, Joanna Scott, and I were unexpectedly living for a few months in Merrill's house in Stonington. We loved the dust of snow, which was fake, laid down for a movie being filmed there. We loved the people of the village, and every day we lived in James Merrill's library: here were the books of our youth, frozen in time, as nothing else was. Assembling this poem about the village, I found myself thinking about its people and, perhaps most of all, about those books, about how thrilling it was to touch them again."

WARREN C. LONGMIRE was born in Philadelphia, Pennsylvania, in 1982. He has released three chapbooks: *Ripped Winters* (Seventh Tangent, 2006), *Do.Until.True.* (Two Pens and Lint, 2012) and *the Wyoming default* (Moonstone Press, 2018). His first full-length collection is *Hooptee* (Radiator Press, 2021).

Of "Meditations on a Photograph of Historic Rail Women," Longmire writes: "The original version of this poem was made within a writing workshop run by Sonia Sanchez during her reign as the first poet laureate of Philadelphia. It was the third day of the workshop, each feeling very loose and as exuberant as the poet herself. From a box she pulled a postcard with a blank back and a small caption I can't remember and passed it around, noting how historic the scene of four Black women doing men's work should feel in our hands. My mind couldn't leave how different the women all looked, how I didn't know any of what brought them to that photo op or what happened after. When speaking of Black folk, I always feel we are cheated in how disconnected we are made from our individuality, even and especially when we are installed as heroes. This logic puzzle of a poem speaks to that."

EMILY LEE LUAN was born in 1992 and raised in Chelmsford, Massachusetts. She is the author of *I Watch the Boughs* (2021), selected by Gabrielle Calvocoressi for a Poetry Society of America Chapbook Fellowship. A 2020 Margins Fellow at the Asian American Writers' Workshop, she holds an MFA in poetry from Rutgers University in Newark.

Of "When My Sorrow Was Born," Luan writes: "I light up when I find a poem that insists on the explicit naming of 'my sorrow' or 'my sadness.' Writing those phrases into a poem can be both gratifying and difficult—simultaneously working against the traditional, apolitical sensibility of 'not telling' and confronting the bald head of your sadness. In Khalil Gibran's poem of the same name, the speaker's sorrow is anthropomorphized and embodied. I love his repetition of and almost absurd insistence on naming Sorrow; the 'and' that begins each line a mirror of grief that appears again and again and again. I began writing after this poem as an exercise in walking with the emotion I most often approach as object. In Gibran's version, the speaker's Sorrow dies and he is left alone. I'm not sure my Sorrow is dead yet, or if our Sorrows ever leave us."

DORA MALECH was born in New Haven, Connecticut, in 1981, and lives in Baltimore, Maryland, where she is on the faculty of The Writing Seminars at Johns Hopkins University. She is the author of the poetry collections *Flourish* (Carnegie Mellon University Press, 2020), *Stet* (Princeton University Press, 2018), *Say So* (Cleveland State University Poetry Center, 2011), and *Shore Ordered Ocean* (The Waywiser Press, 2009). Eris Press (Urtext Ltd.) published *Soundings* (a selected volume of poems and artwork) in the UK in 2019, and Tupelo Press published a chapbook of her poetry titled *Time Trying* in *Four Quartets: Poetry in the Pandemic* in 2020. She has received an Amy Clampitt Residency Award, a Mary Sawyers Baker Prize, a Ruth Lilly Poetry Fellowship, and a residency fellowship from the Civitella Ranieri Foundation.

Of "All the Stops," Malech writes: "This poem belongs not to the storied sweep of American road trip literature, but to the less-sung start-and-stop of the daily commute. It was 'written' first in my mind as a quotidian collection of recurring observations, thoughts, memories, and feelings that began to organize themselves into a map-to-nowhere, or rather, an idiosyncratic map of the interchanges and cul-de-sacs of my mind. Folks familiar with University Parkway in Baltimore might recognize the 'THIS IS YOUR SIGNAL' sign; it's intended to stop absent-minded drivers (and T-bone collisions) at the first of two close traffic lights, but how many of us have idled beneath it and tried to believe it was telling us (à la Rilke) to change our lives? For me, themes of obedience and disobedience cohered at the point of revision—that process that often tells me what has actually been on my mind. And I had to fact-check the final simile with my husband, a film and media studies scholar; I loved the idea of red shapes appearing 'evergreen' on a film negative, but would the era of highly flammable nitrate stock have overlapped with the era of color? His verdict was yes, but the overlap would have been brief. All the poem needed was the possibility, so the figure remained."

SALLY WEN MAO was born in Wuhan, China, in 1987, and was raised in northern California. She is the author of two collections of poetry: *Oculus* (Graywolf Press, 2019), and *Mad Honey Symposium* (Alice James Books, 2014). She has received an NEA fellowship and was recently a Cullman Fellow at the New York Public Library, a Jenny McKean Moore Writer-in-Washington at the George Washington University, and a Shearing Fellow at the Black Mountain Institute. Her work was selected for *The Best American Poetry 2013*. She is a Kundiman fellow in both fiction and poetry.

Of "Playing Dead," Mao writes: "I wrote this poem in 2017, during the autumn rise of #MeToo. At the time, I was grappling with and re-examining aspects of my past. How as I came of age, I internalized and 'accepted' a lot of harmful cultural and societal norms around consent and the treatment of women because apparently that's 'just how it was.' The norms were not a problem, I was the problem for feeling the way I did. I thought back to a situation in college that had caused me a lot of emotional harm, and how there were no resources or support and so I felt compelled to just accept it, and that my feelings didn't matter. Ten years later, I went back and reevaluated that situation and realized that I never gave consent, and my surprise and shock were elements of a violation that I did not know or identify as a violation. The image of the possum is so compelling to me because the possum's fight-or-flight mode parallels the experience of survivors, especially women, who pretend to be dead just to get through or bear something.

Often this pretending fails. Metaphors serve as imperfect conduits to a difficult experience or emotion, and in this case, I was leaning into that metaphor."

FRANCISCO MÁRQUEZ was born in Miami, Florida, in 1994 and raised in Maracaibo, Venezuela. He has received fellowships from the Poetry Project, Tin House, and the Fine Arts Work Center. He is assistant web editor at *Poets & Writers* and lives in Brooklyn, New York.

Of "Provincetown," Márquez writes: "This poem was written during a long, cold winter on a fellowship at the Fine Arts Work Center in Provincetown, Massachusetts. As part of my routine, and as a way of getting out of my own head, I allowed myself to take long walks down the coast every day, often making it to the breakwater, and letting the moving light and landscape fill my head instead. Once I sat down to write, I arranged the observations into a coherent structure and, with very little editing, almost like a gift, the poem came together rather mysteriously. I think the poem served as a kind of deep study of the various themes I had written into at the time, and years before, regarding home, exile, immigration, community, and my relationship to nature. I often feel unsure or unsatisfied with most of what I write, but this poem was one of the few times it felt different, as if some clear, familiar voice had reached its way through."

HANNAH MARSHALL was born in Winfield, Illinois, in 1987, and grew up in the Driftless Area of the Midwest. She currently lives in south-central Illinois, where she works as the advising editor for Greenville University's literary journal, *The Scriblerus*, and as the poetry editor for Converse College's literary journal, *South 85*. She received her MFA in creative writing from Converse College.

Of "This Is a Love Poem to Trees," Marshall writes: "Trees are one of my obsessions. I take pictures of bark and leaves to identify each species. I run my hands over their rough skin, press my ear to their trunks, listen for their voices. I walk my neighborhood cataloguing my companions through each season. The trees, of course, don't love me back, but they tolerate my caresses and grow with imperceptible slowness. When I wrote 'This Is a Love Poem to Trees,' I was at a residency in South Carolina. I wandered the campus, missing my family and reveling in the lush myrtle and oak and magnolia. Even as I found comfort in the trees, they were for me a symbol of longing. I can mark my homes in Minnesota, Wisconsin, and Illinois by tallying the trees that were my friends in these places. I have done so in this poem, tracing my human and ecological love stories through time and space."

SHANE MCCRAE was born in Portland, Oregon, in 1975. His most recent books are *Sometimes I Never Suffered* and *The Gilded Auction Block*, both published by Farrar, Straus and Giroux. In 2021, the Cleveland State University Poetry Center released an expanded edition of his first book, *Mule*, with an introduction by Victoria Chang. McCrae has received an Anisfield-Wolf Book Award, a Guggenheim Fellowship, a Lannan Literary Award, a National Endowment for the Arts Fellowship, and a Whiting Writer's Award. He lives in New York City and teaches at Columbia University.

McCrae writes: "Although 'The Hastily Assembled Angel on Care and Vitality' was selected from *The Yale Review*, where it was published in 2020—for which I will forever be grateful—it was first published in *The Baffler* in 2019, for which I will also forever be grateful. I screwed up, and as a result the poem was accidentally published twice, and I want to acknowledge *The Baffler* for publishing it in the first place. As for the content of the poem, the hastily assembled angel is forever finding himself immobilized by his imperfect understanding of his role as an observer, and, because of this, though all he does, and all he's supposed to do, is observe, imperfectly observing."

Writer, educator, and activist LUPE MENDEZ was born in Galveston, Texas, in 1976. He is the author of the poetry collection *Why I Am Like Tequila* (Willow Books, 2019), winner of the 2019 John A. Robertson award for best first book of poetry from the Texas Institute of Letters. He lives in Houston, where he dedicates energy as the founder of Tintero Projects in addition to working as a public school educator while currently serving as *Poets & Writers'* Literary Outreach Coordinator for Houston.

Of "There Is Only You," Mendez writes: "My daughter, Luz María Magdalena Mendez Rosario, was born in the month of May and when I finally got to bring my parents up from Galveston to Houston to have them see her for the first time, they were all smiles and laughs. My mother must have given her about ten blessings and my dad kept insisting that I take care of my wife and not go out and have a party to celebrate the birth (it was something he did, that all Mexican families used to do, making mothers work extra hard). I distinctly remember as we were leaving so I could take them back down to their car my father called home to Jalisco—to La Pareja, the rancho where my family is from, and he tells my grandfather that he no longer has plans to move us back home to Mexico. He told him, 'My future is here, with this baby. We have our legacy.' As the first Mendez to be born in the U.S., I was taken aback. I always felt like being in between two worlds. But in my father's eyes, I am as immigrant as he is, as Mexican as he and my daughter is something even more. She is all Dominican. She is all Mexican. She is all things."

FRANCINE MERASTY is a Nehithaw Iskwew (Woodland Cree Woman) from Opawikoschikanek (Pelican Narrows), a reserve in Northern Saskatchewan. She is a member of the Peter Ballantyne Cree Nation, a fluent Cree speaker, and is a lawyer and executive assistant at the Federation of Sovereign Indigenous Nations in Saskatchewan. Francine's lived experience as an Indigenous woman from the Pelican Narrows reservation, her memories of the wilderness, her experiences as a residential school survivor, and her current work as a lawyer, all shape her perspective. She began writing poetry in the winter of 2017 while working as a statement taker and legal counsel for the National Inquiry into Missing and Murdered Indigenous Women and Girls. She won a 2019 Indigenous Voices Award. Her first publication, *Iskotew Iskwew: Poetry of a Northern Rez Girl*, was released by Bookland Press in 2021.

Of "Since Time Immemorial," Merasty writes: "I was filling out my law school application in January, 2013, and one of the questions on the application was 'How long has your family lived in Saskatchewan?' Being literally indigenous to Northern Saskatchewan, I really had no idea what to write. As long as the trees? As long as the stars?

"My mind was then flooded with the memory of a traditional hoop dancing group I belonged to as a girl. The group leader who introduced us always began with the story of the dance, and how those measured steps had been taken since 'time immemorial.'

"I looked up the meaning of that phrase in the dictionary: 'a time so long ago that people have no record or knowledge of it.'"

YESENIA MONTILLA is an Afro-Latina poet & a daughter of immigrants. She received her MFA from Drew University in poetry & poetry in translation. She is a CantoMundo graduate and a 2020 New York Foundation for the Arts fellow. *The Pink Box*, her first collection, was published by Willow Books in 2015. Her second collection, *Muse*

Found in a Colonized Body, is forthcoming from Four Way Books in 2022. She lives in Harlem, New York.

Of "a brief meditation on breath," Montilla writes: "2020 was a year in which the breath became politicized by all citizens. I say 'by all' because for Black people in this country the breath has always been political; I am imagining Eric Garner and George Floyd would agree if they were still here. With the pandemic, and mask-wearing becoming the norm, I began to ruminate on how these two circumstances I am living through—being Black in America and existing during a pandemic that literally takes away your breath—could coexist in a poem. In the process of writing it I learned about the ways I take in air, the ways I hold breath, too."

KAMILAH AISHA MOON was born in Nashville, Tennessee, in 1973. She holds an MFA from Sarah Lawrence College. Her books include *Starshine & Clay* (Four Way Books, 2017), and *She Has a Name* (Four Way Books, 2013). She has received fellowships at MacDowell, Vermont Studio Center, and Hedgebrook. She is an assistant professor of poetry and creative writing at Agnes Scott College in Decatur, Georgia.

Of "Irony," Moon writes: "This triolet allows the speaker to lament having no time left to enjoy the rest of a life freed after finally clearing a major existential hurdle."

STANLEY MOSS was born in Woodhaven, New York, on June 21, 1925. He was educated at Trinity College and Yale University, and he served in the U.S. Navy during World War II. After the war he worked at *Botteghe Oscure* and taught English in Rome and Barcelona. His first book of poems, *The Wrong Angel*, was published in 1966, and since then he has also published *The Skull of Adam* (1979), *The Intelligence of Clouds* (1989), *Asleep in the Garden* (1997), *A History of Color* (2003), *Songs of Imperfection* (2005), *New and Selected Poems* (2006), *Rejoicing* (2009), *No Tear is Commonplace* (2013), *It's About Time* (2015), *Almost Complete Poems* (2016), *Abandoned Poems* (2018), *God Breaketh Not All Men's Hearts Alike: New and Selected Poems 1948–2019*, and *Act V, Scene I* (2020). His books have been published in German (tr. by Hans Magnus Enzensberger), Chinese (tr. by Fu Hao), and Spanish (tr. by Valarie Mejer). Moss has worked as an editor at New Directions, New American Library, *Bookweek*, *New York Herald Tribune*, and *New American Review*. In 1977, he founded Sheep Meadow Press, a nonprofit publishing company that publishes poetry and belles lettres. He makes his living as a private art dealer, largely in Spanish and Italian Old Masters. He lives in Clinton Corners, New York.

Of "A Smiling Understanding," Moss writes: "I have a special relationship with trees. At times of sorrow or great difficulty I know trees I love would lend me a helping hand, a branch if they could. I think my trees know I don't want my sap to freeze. That's common sense."

DG NANOUK OKPIK was born in Anchorage, and her family is from Barrow, Alaska. She earned an MFA from the University of Southern Maine's Stonecoast program and is the author of *Corpse Whale* (University of Arizona Press, 2012), which won the American Book Award. Inupiat, Inuit from Alaska, okpik received the Truman Capote Literary Trust Scholarship. An alumna of the Institute of American Indian Arts, she lives in Santa Fe.

Of "When White Hawks Come," okpik writes: "Traveling in dream state, waking up, as fast as I could, to write this piece, in bed. The dream 'sashays' as the poem is in constant movement but 'suspended' in old man forest. I stayed there in the blue night in 'mirth,' rapture, and in laughter."

CECILY PARKS was born in New York in 1976. She is the author of two poetry collections: *Field Folly Snow* (University of Georgia Press, 2008) and *O'Nights* (Alice James Books, 2015). She is the poetry editor of *ISLE: Interdisciplinary Studies in Literature and Environment* and teaches in the MFA program at Texas State University.

Parks writes: "To begin to write 'December,' I looked at all the photographs I'd taken on my phone during the month of December 2017. There they were: the freak Texas snow, children playing on a white bed, masks, a manicure, a note taped to the door, ice skates, ponies, hay, and so on, including a photo of my family's coats piled in an airport lounge on the last day of the month. The draft of Anne Sexton's that the poem refers to is an early version of 'Flee on Your Donkey' and can be found at the Harry Ransom Center at the University of Texas. I love the way Sexton's scrawled declaration, which is in all caps in the original—'AT LAST I FOUND YOU'—reveals how sometimes we write to discover what we're writing."

PATRICK PHILLIPS was born in Atlanta, Georgia, in 1970. He is the author of three books of poems, including *Elegy for a Broken Machine* (Knopf, 2015). His first work of nonfiction, *Blood at the Root: A Racial*

Cleansing in America (W. W. Norton, 2016), won the American Book Award and was named a best book of the year by *The New York Times*, *The Washington Post*, and *Smithsonian*. Phillips teaches writing and literature at Stanford University.

Of "Elegy with Table Saw & Cobwebs," he writes: "This poem grew out of a real experience—the day I first returned to my father-in-law's basement woodshop, and found everything exactly as he'd left it before he died. It's a place where I'd spent many happy hours working and learning from Ollie, an engineer, tinkerer, and jack-of-all-trades, whose shop was waiting like the *Titanic* on the bottom of the sea. Everything dust-covered and frozen in time, with the only difference being that the man himself—the one for whom it all existed—was now gone.

"Like a lot of poems, this one started with astonishment, in its etymological sense of being turned to stone. I felt mute and paralyzed standing in that room, and the only thing I knew for certain was that the experience meant *something*. That it was important. So for me writing the poem wasn't about recording what I'd learned from walking down those steps, but trying to make sense of it.

"I find formal patterns calming and consoling, and almost of its own volition this poem settled into an invented form, with all those *a* sounds repeating at the ends of lines. That wasn't planned, but a way to keep going even as the pressure to stop talking mounted. A way to dwell in a place full of love and memory and loss and, of course, its terrible lesson: that even the most mundane objects might outlive us. My friend Ollie was far too modest for some grand poetic monument. So I tried, at least, to fashion something from scraps."

ROGER REEVES was born and raised in Mount Holly, New Jersey, a small town about forty minutes due east of Philadelphia. He has published one book of poems, *King Me* (Copper Canyon Press, 2013). His next book of poems, *Best Barbarian*, is forthcoming from W. W. Norton in March of 2022.

Of "For Black Children at the End of the World—and the Beginning," Reeves writes: " 'I don't want the police to shoot me,' said L—, a friend's five-year-old child, as they were waiting to participate in a socially distant car-caravan protest that would snake its way through the South Austin streets, a protest aimed at the City Manager and the City Council's recent deliberation over the police budget. Another friend's child, a boy of eight, said the same thing while participating in a protest shortly after the murder of George Floyd, waving at snipers on the roof of the capitol building in hopes that if he waved, the snipers might not shoot him. Some of the snipers waved back. I realized that these black children must be accounted for, loved, considered in the middle of this moment of protesting, in the middle of this fight against white supremacy. I wrote this poem as a turn to them, to the Black children that live in America and have lived in America. I wrote it for all of us."

ED ROBERSON was born on December 26, 1939, in Pittsburgh, Pennsylvania. His most recent of twelve books of poetry are *Asked What Has Changed* (Wesleyan University Press, 2021) and *mph & Other Road Poems* (Verge Publications, 2021). Other titles include *To See the Earth Before the End of the World* (Wesleyan, 2010) and *City Eclogue* (Atelos, 2006).

Of "For Air," Roberson writes: "This poem, with the central image of air, is one of many responding to the senseless police choking murder of George Floyd, but in actuality, it is in response to the numerous unjustified murders of Black people by police force."

MARGARET ROSS was born in New York City in 1986. Her first book, *A Timeshare*, was published by Omnidawn in 2015. The recipient of a Fulbright grant and a Wallace Stegner Fellowship, she currently teaches at the University of Chicago.

Of "Blood," Ross writes: "This poem began as an attempt to write about forms of etiquette shaped by white American fictions, among them the fantasy of linear time in which every present is a blank slate and the past is past."

ANGBEEN SALEEM was born in 1989 in Gujranwala, Pakistan, and was raised in Philadelphia, Pennsylvania. She lives in Brooklyn, New York, and is working on her first collection of poems.

Saleem writes: "I wrote 'brown and black people on shark tank' in a workshop with Angel Nafis and for some reason, it was one of those poems that came to me very quickly. I think it's because part of writing the poem was actually just watching the show *Shark Tank* every Friday night for years and thinking about the ways capitalism requires people of color to sell their trauma, and even that is not always enough. I wanted to capture this notion without being condescending, so that I wasn't attacking people put in these positions, and with a sense of humor, so that I was capturing the absurdity of life under late stage capitalism."

Born in St. Thomas, U.S.V.I. and raised in Apopka, Florida, NICOLE SEALEY is the author of *Ordinary Beast* and *The Animal After Whom Other Animals Are Named*, winner of the Drinking Gourd Chapbook Poetry Prize. She has received the Rome Prize from the American Academy in Rome, a Hodder Fellowship from Princeton University, the Stanley Kunitz Memorial Prize from *The American Poetry Review* and a *Poetry International* Prize, as well as fellowships from the Bread Loaf Writers' Conference, CantoMundo, Cave Canem, MacDowell, the National Endowment for the Arts, the New York Foundation for the Arts, and the Poetry Project. Her work has appeared in *The Best American Poetry 2018*. Formerly the executive director at Cave Canem Foundation, she is a visiting professor at Boston University and Syracuse University.

EVIE SHOCKLEY was born and raised in Nashville, Tennessee. Her most recent poetry collections are *the new black* (Wesleyan, 2011) and *semiautomatic* (Wesleyan, 2017); both won the Hurston/Wright Legacy Award. Her critical work includes her monograph, *Renegade Poetics: Black Aesthetics and Formal Innovation in African American Poetry* (Iowa, 2011). She has received the Lannan Literary Award for poetry, the Stephen Henderson Award, the Holmes National Poetry Prize, and fellowships from the Radcliffe Institute for Advanced Study, MacDowell, and Cave Canem. She is professor of English at Rutgers University.

Of "women's voting rights at one hundred (but who's counting?)," Shockley writes: "I was fortunate to be invited to write a poem for the Academy of American Poets and New York Philharmonic's Project 19, their joint initiative to celebrate the 100th anniversary of the Nineteenth Amendment by commissioning new work from nineteen women poets and nineteen women composers. Though the commission did not place any limits on what I might write about, I was almost immediately drawn to consider the differential meaning of this anniversary for women in terms of race. The delayed access of white women to this important aspect of U.S. citizenship was even further deferred for Black women, who suffered exclusion from the polls on racial grounds, like Black people generally. My poem calls us not only to remember the difference racism made (and continues to make, in numerous ways), but also remember and honor the essential, even heroic, roles played by Black women for more than a century in the ongoing struggle for voting rights—whether in the national spotlight, like Fannie Lou Hamer, or quietly and locally, like Leatha Shockley (my beloved mother!). The formal structure of the poem, its varying discourses, and attention to language, which I enjoyed the challenge of creating, are all in service of illuminating this history and the opportunity we each have to *create* the conditions for freedom and equality."

DARIUS SIMPSON is a writer, educator, performer, and skilled living-room dancer from Akron, Ohio. He was a recipient of the 2020 Ruth Lilly and Dorothy Sargent Rosenberg Poetry Fellowship.

Of "What Is There to Do in Akron, Ohio?" Simpson writes: "This poem was born from a session of poets throwing jokes at me about Ohio and my being from there. During these series of playfully disrespectful comments about my home state someone asked what there even was to do in Ohio."

PATRICIA SMITH was born in Chicago, Illinois, in 1955. She is the author of eight books of poetry, including *Incendiary Art* (Northwestern University Press, 2017), winner of the 2018 Kingsley Tufts Award, the 2017 Los Angeles Times Book Prize, and the 2018 NAACP Image Award; *Shoulda Been Jimi Savannah* (Coffee House Press, 2012), winner of the Lenore Marshall Prize from the Academy of American Poets; and *Blood Dazzler* (Coffee House Press, 2008). She is a Guggenheim fellow, an NEA grant recipient, a former fellow at Civitella Ranieri, Yaddo, and MacDowell, a professor in the MFA program at Sierra Nevada College and at the City University of New York.

Of "The Stuff of Astounding: A Golden Shovel for Juneteenth," Smith writes: "Crafting a commissioned poem is always a tremendous challenge, especially with a topic as expansive as Juneteenth—celebration of the emancipation of our country's enslaved. I wanted the poem to inform the unfamiliar and bolster the spirits of those who can actually trace their beginnings back to those whose shackles were loosed that day. Faced with the daunting task of speaking to everyone about something so utterly necessary, I also wanted to embed a message that spoke resolutely to the present day. After all, it is history that roots us. I decided that the golden shovel, the poetic form created by Terrance Hayes, was the perfect solution. And there's the message, visible when you read down the right side of the poem: 'Unless we are intent on ripping the world from its root in the sky, we live with these truths—

the black breath is gospel, the black voice will not be silent, the black body is free, and black lives matter.' "

MONICA SOK was born in Lancaster, Pennsylvania, in 1990. She is the daughter of Khmer refugees and the granddaughter of Em Bun, a master weaver from Takeo, Cambodia, to whom her first book, *A Nail the Evening Hangs On* (Copper Canyon Press, 2020), is dedicated. Sok has received fellowships from the Poetry Society of America, Hedgebrook, Elizabeth George Foundation, the National Endowment for the Arts, Kundiman, Jerome Foundation, and MacDowell. A Jones Lecturer at Stanford University, Sok teaches poetry to Southeast Asian youths at the Center for Empowering Refugees and Immigrants in Oakland, California.

Of "Ode to the Boy Who Jumped Me," Sok writes: "After this incident I asked myself: What is it like to feel safe, seen, and heard all at once and all the time? In this poem, I wove two complex experiences together (getting jumped/being ghosted), while considering the layers of silence in both. I wrote this as an ode, not to praise the boy who jumped me but to directly address him, to let him know that I saw him that night even when he could not see me."

ADRIENNE SU, born in Atlanta, Georgia, in 1967, is the author of five books of poems: *Peach State* (University of Pittsburgh, 2021), *Living Quarters* (Manic D Press, 2015), *Having None of It* (Manic D, 2009), *Sanctuary* (Manic D, 2006), and *Middle Kingdom* (Alice James Books, 1997). She has received fellowships from the Barbara Deming Fund and the National Endowment for the Arts. She lives in Carlisle, Pennsylvania, where she is professor of creative writing and poet-in-residence at Dickinson College.

Su writes: "By the time I wrote the poem 'Chinese Restaurant Syndrome,' I had been trying to write it for many years. It began in 1999 as an essay on MSG: how I perceived it and how it was perceived in China and the United States. The essay never succeeded, but I couldn't scrap it, as it contained a kernel of irritation that seemed to have potential.

"In 2016, when I started the poem, I was thinking not about the essay but about how much of my early life had been spent in Chinese restaurants. Hosting a Chinese meal at home generally involves last-minute, high-heat cooking of as many dishes as guests, which means the cook, who has probably spent the day cleaning house and prepping ingredients, misses most of the meal. Since Chinese restaurants eliminate this problem, usually at reasonable prices, while offering dishes that are hard to make at home, such as stir-fried lobster, most of the Chinese American gatherings in my life, from casual get-togethers to large family reunions, have been restaurant-centered.

"It felt urgent to get this down because in 2016, many of the elders with whom I had shared those early meals were no longer living or had become too ill to dine out. For the most part, they were also of the generation that had made us Americans. Irritation had given the poem a start, if in the wrong genre. Grief completed it."

ARTHUR SZE was born in New York City in 1950. He is the author of eleven books of poetry, including *The Glass Constellation: New and Collected Poems* (Copper Canyon Press, 2021). His previous book, *Sight Lines* (Copper Canyon, 2019), received the National Book Award for Poetry. A fellow of the American Academy of Arts and Sciences, he is a professor emeritus at the Institute of American Indian Arts.

Of "Acequia del Llano," Sze writes: "In northern New Mexico, acequias are the lifeblood of agriculture and promote sharing of resources and food. During this challenging year with COVID-19, I found my involvement with the Acequia del Llano particularly rewarding. I decided to use the Japanese haibun form to personalize my involvement. The haibun is a form that begins with prose and then interrupts that motion with a haiku, then the prose continues, along with another haiku, and so on. As I wrote 'Acequia del Llano,' I decided to play off these expectations and constraints. Instead of using one haiku after another, I used a 5-7-5 syllable link (this order is broken in one instance) and then a 7-7 syllable link. The two links create the equivalent of a Japanese tanka, a 5-7-5-7-7 syllable form. In writing these links, I wanted to create poems inside of the larger prose poem. In the four sections, each section contains a haiku, a tanka, as well as prose. I see these forms as a way to explore microcosms inside the macrocosm, as a way to create islands inside of a larger flow, and also as a way to aggregate and magnify resonances."

PAUL TRAN was born in San Diego, California, in 1992, and is the author of the debut poetry collection *All the Flowers Kneeling*, forthcoming from Penguin Poets in 2022. Their work has appeared in *The New Yorker* and *Poetry*. A recipient of the Ruth Lilly & Dorothy Sargent Rosenberg Fellowship from the Poetry Foundation and the Discovery/

Boston Review Poetry Prize, Paul is a Wallace Stegner Fellow in poetry at Stanford University.

Tran writes: "I thought suffering made me special. It doesn't. I learned this writing 'Copernicus' forty-five minutes before the class for which I had to assemble a new poem weekly. All I assumed I knew fell away as I typed that opening question, as I realized how misinformed I'd been, my whole life, about my life. Negative capability, then, to me, was the ability to hold opposing truths at once. It became, because of this poem, the ability to annul myself, my received ideas and investments, to arrive at half-knowledge. A poem is a path to knowledge, even if the knowledge is that there's none—none I can live with, none I can be certain about. And I'm grateful to my teachers, Carl Phillips and Mary Jo Bang, in whose class this poem was written, for the education that makes all my poems, and my life, possible."

PHUONG T. VUONG, born in Huế, Vietnam, in 1987, has been awarded fellowships from Tin House, VONA/Voices, and Kearny Street Workshop's Interdisciplinary Writers Lab. She has publications in or forthcoming in *The American Poetry Review*, *Prairie Schooner*, and The Asian American Writers' Workshop: *The Margins*. Her debut poetry collection *The House I Inherit* was released by Finishing Line Press in 2019. Hailing from Oakland, by way of Vietnam, Phuong is pursuing her PhD in literature at the University of California, San Diego, situated on unceded Kumeyaay land, where she researches Asian American feminism and communes with the Pacific, probably with tea on hand.

Of "The Beginning of the Beginning," Vuong writes: "This poem is for Valeria and Óscar Alberto Martínez Ramírez and so many others who risk their lives simply to live."

JOHN SIBLEY WILLIAMS was born in Wilmington, Massachusetts, in 1978. He is the author of five collections, most recently *As One Fire Consumes Another* (Orison Poetry Prize, 2019), *Skin Memory* (Backwaters Prize, University of Nebraska Press, 2019), and *Summon* (Juxta-Prose Chapbook Prize, forthcoming). John has won the Wabash Prize for poetry, Philip Booth Award, Phyllis Smart-Young Prize, and Laux/Millar Prize. He is the editor of *The Inflectionist Review* and founder of the Caesura Poetry Workshop series.

Of "The Dead Just Need to Be Seen. Not Forgiven.," Sibley writes: "The often-violent collision of family history, privilege, and how our ghosts continue to linger and influence us motivated me to write this narrative poem about the most basic form of acceptance: recognizing our impotence to change the past. I've long been haunted by Shakespeare's line, 'The sins of the father are to be laid upon the children.' Is it true that burden, guilt, and responsibility migrate through blood lines? What should one do when encountering the spirit of a dead relative whose perspective and actions were aggressively different than one's own? I have no answers here, only questions which lead to other questions."

L. ASH WILLIAMS was born in Brooklyn, New York, in 1985. She was Host Committee Chair for the 2016 Women of the World Poetry Slam (WOWPs) and was a member of the 2013 louderARTS National Poetry Slam team. L. Ash has most recently been featured at Bowery Poetry, SupaDupaFresh, and the Nuyorican Poets Cafe. Her work has been published by the American Public Media (*The Slowdown* podcast, 2020).

Of "Red Wine Spills," Williams writes: "I wrote this poem because a typically benign experience became a stand-out moment in my day. Spills happen often, but there was something about this one—the 'of course' moment when I knocked the glass over; the wave of negative self-thought that rolled in once it happened; the utter relief I felt once the stain disappeared. My attachment to the moment was alarming. This piece helped me explore what I was feeling and gave me a way to move through it."

SHELLEY WONG was born in Long Beach, California, in 1980. Her debut full-length collection, *As She Appears* (YesYes Books, 2022), won the 2019 Pamet River Prize. She has received fellowships from Kundiman, MacDowell, and the Vermont Studio Center. An affiliate artist at Headlands Center for the Arts, she lives in San Francisco.

Of "How to Live in Southern California," Wong writes: "This braided poem was a departure and led me to write more poems about California as a place, environment, and space for meditating on my family's history. Shout-out to my mother's caution, my father's love for Fleetwood Mac, my sister's LA savvy, the off-price Givenchy sunglasses I wore during high school for an Audrey Hepburn glow. To Frank Ocean for being himself and born in Long Beach. In using a braided form, I wanted to resist detachment and America's denial. In SoCal, you can become numb in that clear, blinding light, losing your sense of reality with so much visual distraction and a strange sense of seasonless time. And similarly, one often feels helpless against global warming and attempts to write about it.

"As a result of anti-Asian immigration laws that endured until 1965, most Asian Americans of my generation are second generation, so it comes as a surprise to people that I am fourth generation. I reference this history to speak to the bravery and vulnerability of my eight great-grandparents who persevered through the Chinese Exclusion and Page Acts, and, to quote Ronald Takaki, insist on 'a larger memory of America's past.' The poem took on greater resonance in 2020 with another president promoting anti-Asian hate and violence and the largest wildfire season in California history. As of January 2021, the National Drought Mitigation Center reports that 100 percent of California is abnormally dry, 95 percent is experiencing moderate drought, 74 percent severe drought, 34 percent extreme drought, and 1 percent exceptional drought."

JOHN YAU was born in Lynn, Massachusetts, in 1950. His most recent books of poetry are *Bijoux in the Dark* (Letter Machine Editions, 2018) and *Genghis Chan on Drums* (Omnidawn, 2021). In 2020, MadHat published *Foreign Sounds or Sounds Foreign*, a selection of his reviews and essays. He is the 2018 recipient of the Jackson Poetry Prize. A cofounder of the online magazine *Hyperallergic Weekend*, where his reviews appear regularly, he teaches at Mason Gross School of the Arts and lives in Manhattan.

Yau writes: "I wrote 'Overnight' in memory of the poet Paul Violi. In his poems, Paul often worked in arcane forms as well as invented his own, including ones that mimicked a glossary, an index, and an errata sheet. The form I used is a pantoum, which is written in four-line stanzas, with each line in the stanza repeated twice in a strict order. In 'Overnight,' I divided the four-line stanza into two-line stanzas. I wanted to call further attention to the repetitions, as well as discover what happened as the lines changed position in the pairing. I felt that writing in this form, which is half-invented, honored Paul's love of poetic forms, as well as got at his humor and my powerlessness to change the situation."

MONICA YOUN was born In Berkeley, California, in 1971, and was raised in Houston, Texas. She is the author of *Blackacre* (Graywolf Press, 2016), *Ignatz* (Four Way Books, 2010), and *Barter* (Graywolf Press, 2003).

Of "Caution," Youn writes: "This poem is part of a series titled 'Deracinations: Seven Sonigrams.' Many of the key words of the poems are 'sonigrams' of the word 'deracinations'—that is, they contain the sounds or letters of the source word. I created the term 'sonigram' because I wanted a form that was more fluid than the anagram—more of a sonic landscape than a strict mathematical permutation. 'Deracinations' is a subtle-sounding word, Latinate, made up of commonplace sounds—for me, this mirrored the everyday effects of deracination, which are often barely perceptible but, nonetheless, omnipresent."

KEVIN YOUNG was born in 1970. He is the author of fourteen books of poetry and prose, including *Stones* (Knopf, 2021), where "Dog Tags" also appears. He is the editor of nine other collections, most recently *African American Poetry: 250 Years of Struggle & Song* (Library of America, 2020), named one of the best books of 2020 by *The New York Times*, *Esquire*, *The Atlantic*, *The Chicago Tribune*, *Good Morning America*, and *O, The Oprah Magazine*. A member of the American Academy of Arts and Sciences as well as the American Society of Arts and Letters, Young was the guest editor of *The Best American Poetry 2011*. He was named a Chancellor of the Academy of American Poets in 2020. He is the poetry editor of *The New Yorker* and the Andrew W. Mellon Director of the Smithsonian's National Museum of African American History & Culture in Washington, D.C.

Young writes: " 'Dog Tags' is one of the chief reasons for *Stones* to exist. Visiting the two cemeteries in Louisiana that hold most of my dead is a ritual I had just undertaken when this poem took place. Visiting those centuries-old resting places meant seeing names familiar and lost, and trying to conjure up those who I knew and grew up with, including my cousin whose story underpins the poem. I was struck not only by the pain of her passing too young, but also its odd resemblance to myth—and the ways that poems try to make myth out of life. Or at least that's the Black and blues approach that draws me again and again: naming pain, and plainly, in order to move artfully past it. Looking at it now, I think the poem was wise to give my mother the last words."

MAGAZINES WHERE THE POEMS
WERE FIRST PUBLISHED

The Academy of American Poets Poem-a-Day, guest eds. Mahogany L. Browne, Dana Levin, January Gill O'Neil, Roger Reeves. www.poets.org

Alaska Quarterly Review, ed. Ronald Spatz. www.aqreview.org

The American Poetry Review, ed. Elizabeth Scanlon. www.aprweb.org

American Poets, www.poets.org

The American Scholar, poetry ed. Langdon Hammer. www.theamerican scholar.org

The Art Section, editor-in-chief Deanna Sirlin. www.theartsection.com

The Atlantic, poetry ed. David Barber. www.theatlantic.com

The Believer, poetry ed. Jericho Brown. www.believermag.com

Bennington Review, ed. Michael Dumanis. www.benningtonreview.org

The Brooklyn Rail, poetry ed. Anselm Berrigan. www.brooklynrail.org

The Common, poetry ed. John Hennessy. www.thecommononline.org

Five Points, ed. Megan Sexton. www.fivepoints.gsu.edu

Freeman's, ed. John Freeman. www.freemansbiannual.com

Green Mountains Review, poetry ed. Elizabeth A. I. Powell. www.green mountainsreview.com

Hambone, ed. Nathaniel Mackey. www.fromasecretlocation.com/hambone/

The Kenyon Review, poetry ed. David Baker. www.kenyonreview.org

Literary Hub, editor-in-chief Jonny Diamond. www.lithub.com

The Nation, poetry ed. Kaveh Akbar. www.thenation.com

New England Review, poetry ed. Rick Barot. www.nereview.com

New Ohio Review, ed. David Wanczyk. www.newohioreview.org

The New York Review of Books, executive ed. Jana Prikryl. www.nybooks.com

The New York Times, www.nytimes.com

The New Yorker, poetry ed. Kevin Young. www.newyorker.com

Orion Magazine, poetry ed. Camille T. Dungy. www.orionmagazine.org

The Paris Review, poetry ed. Vijay Seshadri. www.theparisreview.org

Pigeon Pages, poetry ed. Madeleine Mori. www.pigeonpagesnyc.com

Ploughshares, poetry ed. John Skoyles. www.pshares.org

Poetry, eds. Fred Sasaki, Lindsay Garbutt, and Holly Amos. www.poetryfoundation.org/poetrymagazine

The Southampton Review, poetry ed. Cornelius Eady. www.thesouthamptonreview.com

Southern Indiana Review, poetry eds. Emily Skaja and Marcus Wicker. www.usi.edu/sir

The Southern Review, poetry ed. Jessica Faust. www.thesouthernreview.org

The Threepenny Review, ed. Wendy Lesser. www.threepennyreview.com

World Literature Today, Black Voices feature ed. Mahtem Shiferraw. www.worldliteraturetoday.org

The Yale Review, ed. Meghan O'Rourke. www.yalereview.yale.edu

ACKNOWLEDGMENTS

The series editor thanks Mark Bibbins for his invaluable assistance. Warm thanks go also to Angela Ball, Marc Cohen, Amy Gerstler, Stacey Harwood, Major Jackson, Jamie Katz, Mary Jo Salter, and Terence Winch; to Glen Hartley and Lynn Chu of Writers' Representatives; and to Kathy Belden, David Stanford Burr, Daniel Cuddy, Erich Hobbing, and Rosie Mahorter at Scribner. The poetry editors of the magazines that were our sources deserve applause; they are the secret heroes of contemporary poetry.

Grateful acknowledgment is made of the magazines in which these poems first appeared and the magazine editors who selected them. A sincere attempt has been made to locate all copyright holders. Unless otherwise noted, copyright to the poems is held by the individual poets.

Rosa Alcalá, "The Pyramid Scheme" from *Green Mountains Review*. Reprinted by permission of the poet.

Lauren K. Alleyne, "Divination" from *Orion Magazine*. Reprinted by permission of the poet.

Jabari Asim, "Some Call It God" from Poem-a-Day. Reprinted by permission of the poet.

Joshua Bennett, "Benediction" from *Literary Hub*. Reprinted by permission of the poet.

Destiny O. Birdsong, "love poem that ends at popeyes" from *Negotiations*. © 2020 by Destiny O. Birdsong. Reprinted by permission of Tin House Books. Also appeared in *The Kenyon Review*.

Susan Briante, "Further Exercises" from *Defacing the Monument*. © 2020 by Susan Briante. Reprinted by permission of Noemi Press. Also appeared in *The Brooklyn Rail*.

Jericho Brown, "Work" from *The Art Section*. Reprinted by permission of the poet.

Christopher Buckley, "After Tu Fu" from *Five Points*. Reprinted by permission of the poet.

Victoria Chang, "Marfa, Texas" from *New England Review*. Reprinted by permission of the poet.

Nancy Miller Gomez, "Tilt-A-Whirl" from *New Ohio Review*. Reprinted by permission of the poet.

Jorie Graham, "I Won't Live Long" from *Runaway*. © 2020 by Jorie Graham. Reprinted by permission of Ecco/HarperCollins. Also appeared in *The New Yorker*.

Rachel Eliza Griffiths, "Hunger" from *Seeing the Body*. © 2020 by Rachel Eliza Griffiths. Reprinted by permission of W. W. Norton & Co. Also appeared in *The Paris Review*.

francine j. harris, "Sonata in F Minor, K. 183: Allegro" from *Here Is the Sweet Hand*. © 2020 by francine j. harris. Reprinted by permission of Farrar, Straus and Giroux. Also appeared in *The New York Review of Books*.

Terrance Hayes, "George Floyd" from *The New Yorker*. Reprinted by permission of the poet.

Edward Hirsch, "Waste Management" from *Five Points*. Reprinted by permission of the poet.

Ishion Hutchinson, "David" from *The New York Review of Books*. Reprinted by permission of the poet.

Didi Jackson, "Two Mule Deer" from *The Kenyon Review*. Reprinted by permission of the poet.

Major Jackson, "Double Major" from *The Yale Review*. Reprinted by permission of the poet.

Amaud Jamaul Johnson, "So Much for America" from *The Southern Review*. Reprinted by permission of the poet.

Yusef Komunyakaa, "Wheelchair" from *The Paris Review*. Reprinted by permission of the poet.

Dana Levin, "Immigrant Song" from *The Nation*. Reprinted by permission of the poet.

Ada Limón, "The End of Poetry" from *The New Yorker*. Reprinted by permission of the poet.

James Longenbach, "In the Village" from *Forever*. © 2021 by James Longenbach. Reprinted by permission of W. W. Norton & Co. Also appeared in *The American Poetry Review*.

Warren C. Longmire, "Meditations on a Photograph of Historic Rail Women" from *The American Poetry Review*. Reprinted by permission of the poet.

Emily Lee Luan, "When My Sorrow Was Born" from *New Ohio Review*. Reprinted by permission of the poet.

Dora Malech, "All the Stops" from *The Southampton Review*. Reprinted by permission of the poet.

counting?)" from Poets.org and *American Poets*. Reprinted by permission of the poet.

Darius Simpson, "What Is There to Do in Akron, Ohio?" from *New Ohio Review*. Reprinted by permission of the poet.

Patricia Smith, "The Stuff of Astounding: A Golden Shovel for Juneteenth" from *The New York Times*. Reprinted by permission of the poet.

Monica Sok, "Ode to the Boy Who Jumped Me" from Poem-a-Day. Reprinted by permission of the poet.

Adrienne Su, "Chinese Restaurant Syndrome" from *Peach State*. © 2021 by Adrienne Su. Reprinted by permission of the University of Pittsburgh Press. Also appeared in *Bennington Review*.

Arthur Sze, "Acequia del Llano" from *The Glass Constellation: New and Collected Poems*. © 2021 by Arthur Sze. Reprinted by permission of The Permissions Company, Inc. on behalf of Copper Canyon Press. Also appeared in *The Kenyon Review*.

Paul Tran, "Copernicus" from *The New Yorker*. Reprinted by permission of the poet.

Phuong T. Vuong, "The Beginning of the Beginning" from *The American Poetry Review*. Reprinted by permission of the poet.

John Sibley Williams, "The Dead Just Need to Be Seen. Not Forgiven." From *Southern Indiana Review*. Reprinted by permission of the poet.

L. Ash Williams, "Red Wine Spills" from Poem-a-Day. Reprinted by permission of the poet.

Shelley Wong, "How to Live in Southern California" from *The Kenyon Review*. Reprinted by permission of the poet.

John Yau, "Overnight" from *Hambone*. Reprinted by permission of the poet.

Monica Youn, "Caution" (from "Deracinations: Seven Sonigrams") from *Ploughshares*. Reprinted by permission of the poet.

Kevin Young, "Dog Tags" from *Stones*. © 2021 by Kevin Young. Reprinted by permission of Alfred A. Knopf. Also appeared in *Ploughshares*.